design your life

IN BEAUTIFUL & MEANINGFUL WAYS

design your life

IN BEAUTIFUL & MEANINGFUL WAYS

JEFF & RHONNA FARRER

CFI

An imprint of Cedar Fort, Inc.
Springville, Utah

© 2021 Jeff and Rhonna Farrer
All rights reserved.

ISBN 13: 978-1-4621-3794-7

Published by CFI, an imprint of Cedar Fort, Inc.
2373 W. 700 S., Springville, UT 84663
Distributed by Cedar Fort, Inc., www.cedarfort.com

Library of Congress Control Number: 2020952244

Cover design by Rhonna Farrer and Shawnda T. Craig
Cover design © 2021 Cedar Fort, Inc.
Edited and typeset by Valene Wood

Printed in the United States of America

10 9 8 7 6 5 4 3 2 1

Printed on acid-free paper

Dedicated to Jaya, Tali, Kyle, Sol, Rachel, and Corey.
We love you.

Contents

Introduction

---

*In the quiet of an early morning, **honesty** finds me. It calls to me through a crack in my soul and invites the real me to come out, come out, wherever you are. Not the carefully edited edition of the me I am this year. No, honesty wants to speak to the least tidy version of the woman I've become. The one I can't make look more alive with a few swipes of mascara and a little color on my lips.*

—Lysa TerKeurst[1]

IN 1997 WE WERE PREGNANT WITH OUR SECOND CHILD AND FOR some reason we decided to sit down and set some long-term goals as a couple. You have to understand that neither one of us was very goal oriented, so this was a big deal and a bit of a novelty for us. We mapped out where we would be and what we would have accomplished in one year, five, ten, fifteen, and twenty years. Looking back, we can now see what a pivotal moment that was, but even at the time, there was an energy that we both felt as we created these images of the future. It felt important and sacred. We still look back on that moment with reverence. It was the creation of a path, or paths, we would both travel. Sometimes we would travel together and sometimes our paths were quite a bit different, but they were leading us, as long as we stuck to them, to those same goals and others that were created along the way.

---

1. Lysa TerKeurst, *Uninvited: Living Loved When You Feel Less Than, Left Out, and Lonely* (United States: Thomas Nelson, 2016).

This book is part of that journey and it tells, not only our story on that journey, but some of the principles that we found served us as well. We are *not* experts at making and keeping goals; not experts at marriage or raising a family; not experts at life coaching or giving advice. We are not even experts at the principles we are about to discuss, but we *are* experts at how those principles apply to us and our experiences. We are also experts at *our own* self-improvement. The principles in this book are presented generally, but we tell our stories alongside the principles to illustrate how two people made them work, with beautiful results. If the principles are new to you, we know that you too can use them to enrich your life in beautiful and meaningful ways. If the principles are familiar, we hope you enjoy reading of our experiences and maybe you will find new ways to apply familiar principles to improve your own life experiences.

First, some introductions: I would consider myself an artist in the traditional sense. I design and create images on a page, a canvas, a wall, or—these days—a monitor. My husband, Jeff, would describe himself as a scientist. He actually works as an electron microscopist doing research and teaching others how to use the microscopes to do their research. Our interests are often so very different, I find it pretty amazing that we could even agree on the principles of this book, let alone write it together. The paths that brought us both to this point also look very different, and we both recognize that we are probably not at the same point, but we are very "proximal," and so grateful for our own and each other's different journey and different ideas and perspectives.

This work is the combination of years of developing practices both individually and together that have allowed us to recognize the power that we have in designing our own lives and creating within them meaning and purpose. As we have practiced these principles and shared some with friends and family members, we have realized that these principles are universal truths that apply to all of God's children. And the practices or application of these principles, which act to strengthen them within us, are also applicable to all. These fundamental ideas, that Jeff and I agree upon so strongly, are what make this collaboration possible.

Rhonna's Story

I grew up intuitively feeling like I was a creative soul. My grandpa was a photographer and my granny was the original "foodie." Their three children all went into "creative" careers and all were successful in those careers. I thought, as their oldest granddaughter, surely I inherited some of that creative substance, right? Don't creative genes run in the family? My dad, mom, grandpa, and granny always told me I was creative. I enjoyed the thoughts that I was creative and soon I was involved in activities that would confirm and reinforce those thoughts that I was a "creative." When I was a young teenager, my mother took a calligraphy course and I'd watch her practice her new-found love of writing words over and over to get the strokes down just right. I loved how she held the pen, positioning the nib to get the perfect calligraphic angle. I remember my mom teaching me some of the things she had learned about the up and down strokes, nib angle, and styles of calligraphy. I'd sneak into her calligraphy books, papers, pens, and ink and I'd play for hours. I loved writing words, looking at the styles in the book and then creating my own style. When my mom found my practice sheets, she was amazed at my ability and gave me encouragement. I felt so proud of my handwriting skills and continued to write, create, and share my masterpieces with as many people as were willing to accept.

I would cut out pictures from magazines, collage them together and create humorous homemade cards with my greetings, sentiments, and inside jokes for all my friends. They loved them, and I loved that they loved them. It gave me a sense of uniqueness and love that friends and family would ask me to create the birthday posters, student government flyers, or welcome home banners because I was so "creative." I felt such a spark of joy and excitement as I created art pieces that brought cheer to others and connected with my creative self and others. At the time, I really felt like I was born to create and shine as an artist. I felt this peace and sense of self when I was creating. I can now see how my Heavenly Father was nudging my spirit and letting me know: *Yes, you are a Creator. Your spirit finds great joy in creating because it is your innate gift as my daughter*

I didn't know it at the time, in fact it would take years before I recognized it, but I was also learning myths about creativity and those myths were being reinforced in me every time I had some small success as an artist. The first myth is that "creativity" is like a substance and some people have more of it and some less and some maybe not at all. Variants of this myth are that creativity is a characteristic or personality trait that is inherited from parents or ancestors that were also creative or that it is something that is used by artists, craftsmen, entertainers, and imaginative people, and that rest of us don't have it, so we just do repetitive or routine or non-original work.

The second myth is that creativity always results in something that is performed on an instrument or on a stage; displayed in a frame, vase, plate, or pedestal; recorded in a book or read from a page. Of course, if someone has a knack, gift, or talent for creating one of those things, then the myth usually works for them. If not, it may just keep a person from doing something amazing.

The creativity myths can also be detrimental to those that feel they *are* creative. If a creator dangerously compares her work to that of another creator, or receives criticism for which she is not prepared, she may go away feeling that she is not really that "good" and perhaps not creative at all. She may be discouraged from further participation or enjoyment in that activity. I still remember distinctly my mom and I were coloring on opposite sides of a Holly Hobby Coloring book and I was intently coloring what I thought was the most beautiful masterpiece I'd ever created. I remember putting my whole five-year-old heart and soul into it and as I looked up, feeling pretty good about my creation, my jaw dropped when I saw my mom's masterpiece. The color combination was stunning. Even my young eyes could see the beauty she had created with her color palette of choice: yellow, pink, orange, and lime green. My heart sunk. My coloring page wasn't as beautiful as hers. When I expressed my disappointment in my own creation, I remember my mom lovingly assuring me that my coloring page was indeed a masterpiece because of the heart and soul I put into it. With some encouragement and love I realized that yes, my page was indeed a masterpiece.

As a senior in high school, I enrolled in an art class and was enjoying my experience until one day my teacher let me know I would never amount to anything as an artist. I just didn't have what it took. My heart was smashed into pieces. I really took this to heart and believed my teacher. I lost the fire to create. I determined I was supposed to do something else, that I was wrong about my creativity.

I let this limiting belief crush my spirit and dictate what I did for the next few years, until I had an experience where I started to believe again that I *was* born to create *and* to shine as an artist. I allowed my spirit to connect with the Holy Ghost and chose to believe that truth.

I decided to get a degree in Art Education so I could become an art teacher who would encourage others to connect, create beauty, and learn the importance of creative exploration and play. I was determined to see the Creator in each of my students.

During my schooling and even while teaching, I learned I still had to work at overcoming those limiting beliefs brought about by the myths of creativity. Sometimes they would creep back into my heart and I would second guess myself, especially when I'd stand up in front of my college art classes to talk about my artwork and the criticisms seemed harsh; or I wouldn't get the validation of my beautiful creation. It wasn't easy, and there was always this question of what it looked like to be successful as an artist, but deep down, way deep down, I heard my spirit answering the call of my heart and I persevered.

I ended my teaching journey to start our family. Jeff and I loved being parents, and we loved our married life. He was busy in graduate school and I was home with our two little girls that were sixteen months apart. I loved being a mother. I felt so much satisfaction as I nurtured and loved our babies. I felt fulfillment as I created a home filled with the Spirit. I loved molding our little family's daily lives into something magical and wonderful. I didn't see it as clearly then, but I was creating. Admittedly, it was outside of the medium to which I was accustomed, but every moment I was creating a beautiful life for our little girls and Jeff and me.

There were many moments, however, when I felt like my creativity was shriveling up. I missed creating artwork and I felt drawn back to that creative outlet I loved so much.

As Jeff was getting his doctorate, we had a small living stipend from the University, so our budget was tight and we chose to be so frugal. We made our own baby wipes, napkins and Q-tips were a luxury, and I only wore make-up to church on Sundays so I could use the money on things like diapers and food. I got little side jobs occasionally that would supplement our tiny stipend while allowing me to stay home with our babies. We lived in Minnesota at the time, and through a colleague of Jeff's, I got this job stuffing felt horns for hats that fans of the Minnesota Vikings would wear. I remember one night, when the girls were asleep and Jeff was still at school, I was tired, my hands were cracked and bleeding from the amount of cheap filling I had to stuff into hundreds of horns and I sat back on our couch, looked at the huge pile of horns I'd stuffed and started to cry.

I wasn't feeling much satisfaction and fulfillment in that moment. I didn't feel like much of a Creator. From my patriarchal blessing I knew God had given me talents to "build up His kingdom." I couldn't help but ask, was stuffing horns one of my talents? Whose kingdom was I building? I felt pretty low and said a prayer in my heart asking God to show me what He had in store for me when He admonished me to use my talents to build His kingdom. I didn't get the answer right then. In fact, it took me a while to see how all the pieces fit together.

I'm pretty sure it was a mixture of postpartum depression, exhaustion caused by having two babies ages 1 month and 17 months, the stress of serving as the president of the Church's young women organization, and my husband being absent 12 to 14 hours a day, but I was *not* feeling creative nor connected. I shared my feelings of discouragement with Jeff. He listened and asked me, "Well, what do you want to do?" I wasn't sure how to answer that question. So, he clarified and said, "Forget money. If money were no object and you had all the time and resources at your disposal, what would you want to do?" I was still reluctant to say it, but he pressed as if he knew there was something I wanted to say. "Just say it!"

"I want to design my own line of greeting cards!" I blurted out. And Jeff responded, as if it was the simplest most obvious thing in the world, "Then, make it happen." And that started the journey of Rhonna Designs.

Over the years that have passed since that day, I have felt my soul cracked open again and again through experiences of rejection, illness, loss, and change in my life. I have chosen to look inside and be truly honest with myself and recognize what success looked like in *my* life— not others'. I got to embrace the messy, imperfectly perfect *me*. I got to step into authentic power and see my gifts, talents, and abilities as my own divine gift from a loving Heavenly Father. I got to see how I could invite my spirit, my True Self to shine and serve the world. *This* is when I came alive. *This* is when I started feeling "successful." This connection to my True Self has been a process, but I'm learning how to fill the measure of my creation as I learn to turn my heart to God and connect with Him. It is a continual journey and it is beautiful.

Jeff's Story

I wasn't always a scientist. When I was very young, I remember dreaming of being a writer. I loved reading and was fascinated by the ability the authors had of crafting a story and keeping me engrossed. I had an extremely active imagination, so the author's job of keeping me interested was an easy one. Still, I loved writing little short stories that were simply regurgitations or "remixes" of stories from the books I was reading, but you gotta start somewhere, right? As I got older, I learned from just about everyone on the planet, (I think they actually took a poll, and it was unanimous) that I just wouldn't make a lot of money as a writer and I wouldn't be able to support a family, so I shelved my dream.

Part of the problem was that I wanted to make a lot of money. As many people do, I saw that as my pathway to happiness, success, joy, and ease, blah blah blah. And then at some point, I must have ditched that idea too, because I chose to go to graduate school in materials science and engineering.

OK, I'm really getting ahead of myself. Let's back up.

When I met Rhonna, we were both undergraduates at Brigham Young University. I was majoring in Physics, living with my parents, and commuting to campus. Rhonna was studying Art Education, living with roommates close to campus, and knew probably everyone that wasn't in the Physics Department. I was so drawn to her free spirit and her authenticity. Her love and kindness were so real and flowed so easily. I felt inside that I had found a spiritual partner, with whom I could share my innermost thoughts and my life's progression, and I knew she would love me without judgment. And she did.

We were married mid-semester (I don't recommend this to anyone), and I felt we were a perfect fit. She was the creative, follow-your-heart type, and I was the logical, follow-the-data type. When we packed up a rental truck and went off to graduate school with our first child, I had no idea what we were doing or what I was getting us into, so I stuck on a brave face . . . and never took it off.

The brave face became part of my personality. I'm sure I took it off every once in a while, but it seemed to work so well. The family could thrive with a confident, logical, emotionless captain steering the ship, right? But as time passed, I became more cynical and skeptical of things, more hardened and less willing to show emotion. I started to believe the myth that displaying emotion is a sign of weakness. I was also believing the myths about creativity and I was more and more convinced that if I had any at all, it was now dried up and gone.

Several years ago, I felt it was time to make a change. The desire was there, but not the knowledge of how I could make it happen. I prayed a great deal and was led by the Spirit—baby steps at a time— back to a feeling of openness, authentic power, and love. I remember a time, after I had started this journey of change, when we were visited by one of Rhonna's beautiful, outspoken nieces. A few moments after observing me, she said, "What's with 'New Jeff?'" We laughed and talked about the changes she was seeing. Later, when I reflected on what she had said, I openly wept with gratitude, knowing that the changes I was feeling inside were real and noticeable in my behavior. That same niece's father later told me, "I don't like the 'New Jeff' moniker that my daughter uses. I believe it's 'True Jeff.'" He was right, and I felt his words sink deep into my core. I wept with gratitude again. It felt as though I had come back from a long absence.

My relationship with Rhonna went through some changes as well, some easy and some not so easy, but after the dust settled and she was confident that the changes in me were permanent, our relationship became the true spiritual partnership it was always meant to be. I love having a partner that knows what I'm feeling and when I'm not at my best and is able, and willing, to say the words that allow me to get myself back to a space of wisdom, love, and creativity.

We realized that the principles that she had been studying as part of her practice to stay open and creative, were the same principles that had brought about such drastic changes in me. We found that many of our practices to refine and strengthen those principles were overlapping. We compared notes on our practices. We watched and learned from each other. We discussed what worked for each of us and what did not. Our practices are still different in many ways, but the underlying principles that are working to keep us feeling the joy of life and creation are identical.

I still have moments that I feel old patterns and old habits slip back into my behavior, but this journey of continual change has taught me that one of the greatest gifts that God has given me is my agency. With it I have the power not only to choose which path to take but to choose to create a new one. One with beauty, forgiveness, gratitude, and meaning.

The Myths of Creativity

Now that you know a little about us. I want to talk about some things that both of us have gotten hung up on, at one point or another. I actually mentioned this while relating some of my story, but it would serve to review and to clarify what I mean by "limiting beliefs" and the "myths of creativity." These are beliefs that keep us from recognizing truths about ourselves and each other.

The first one is that creativity is an unchangeable characteristic that you were born with. Maybe it was passed down from a parent or grandparent or it runs in the family.

Another is that creativity is a sort of substance or energy of limited quantity within us or similarly that each person has a limited capacity for creativity. Some people have more than others, and sometimes it runs out and you get stuck until you replenish it.

Finally, there is the myth that creativity must result in a work of some kind and it is usually part of the visual or performing arts.

Of course, not everyone believes in these myths, but in many ways they have been incorporated into the way we describe something or someone:

Oh, she's the creative person on the team.

Don't have him run the numbers, he's more of a "creative."

You wrote that? Wow, you must be very creative.

It's a very creative piece.

I was never good at science, I'm more of a creative type.

I feel like I just need to go do something creative.

The Truth About Creativity

So, what is the truth? The truth is that we are *all* creative. We are creative beings. It's part of being human. What gets passed down, or what you might be born with, are talents or aptitudes for specific skills. Now these skills may lead you into artistic fields, but they are *not* what make you a creative person. Your birth into mortality is what made you a creative person. Even when we look at the works of a great artist and say, "That person is creative," we are only looking at a tiny sliver of their life. Sure, they paint, or they write, or they perform, (and I'm not downplaying their accomplishments) but they are still human and they are still involved, like you and me, in progressing through life.

Now if I consider myself a "creative type," then it would seem that this myth works for me. But what happens when the overwhelming argument comes in from that first harsh critic, that what I have created is garbage and I have failed as a creator. Now the myth tells me that maybe I was wrong all along, maybe I'm not part of the creative group as I had thought. My belief in the myth just destroyed my belief in myself as a creative person.

Comparison to others is what the second myth engenders. Many times I have compared my work with that of another, only to come away thinking that I was not as creative as them. This is patently false. We all have an infinite well from which to create thoughts. We all have different skills and aptitudes, and we are all on different points in the learning process. Best of all, we each have different ways that we express the creativity inside of us. This is called creation, and the results are as varied as the people that create them.

Then the final myth is just as untrue. It is not for me to say that less or more creativity exists in the ceiling of the Sistine Chapel than in the design and build of a farm tractor, or in the composition of a letter I received from my brother.

In a talk in 2008, Dieter F. Uchtdorf said:

> The desire to create is one of the deepest yearnings of the human soul. No matter our talents, education, backgrounds, or abilities, we each have an inherent wish to create something that did not exist before. Everyone can create. You don't need money, position, or influence in order to create something of substance or beauty. Creation brings deep satisfaction and fulfillment. . . . The bounds of creativity extend far beyond the limits of a canvas or a sheet of paper and do not require a brush, a pen, or the keys of a piano. Creation means bringing into existence something that did not exist before.[2]

So, what is creativity? The ability to create or the act of creation?

Creativity is in everything. Bottles of homemade yogurt, words in my journal, or the way I do my hair. But more than that, creativity is actually in my thoughts. A thought is creation. Scientist and philosopher, Gary Zukav explained, "A thought is energy, or Light, that has been shaped by consciousness."[3] Anyone that's had a thought is endowed with creativity. Even if the thought is not original, I'm still taking raw material and creating a form—creating matter, however refined. Speech is also a form of creation. Forming *words* is creation. It could be thought of as the next level of creation after a thought. I create something that wasn't there before: the sound (and meaning) of a word.

All of my actions, then, are also creations. The movements of my body as I sit next to someone or give a hug, that is also creativity. Even if I am mimicking something, I am still creating something that wasn't there before: creating something new.

I have learned why it is so important to know this and dispel the myths surrounding creativity: We are all Gods in training. I am

2. Dieter F. Uchtdorf, "Happiness, Your Heritage," *Ensign*, November 2008.
3. Gary Zukav, *The Seat of the Soul* (United States: Simon & Schuster, 1989), 89.

a creative being and everything I do is an act of creation that either brings me closer to God and closer to my divine role or it takes me further from Him, further from my divine role and further from my True Self. When the resurrected Jesus Christ introduces Himself to the people on the American Continent, He immediately points out His role as creator: "Behold, I am Jesus Christ the Son of God. I created the heavens and the earth, and all things that in them are" (3 Nephi 9:15). And while He was on the earth, He was ever careful of the moments He was creating. He taught in the temple at Jerusalem, "I do nothing of myself; but as my Father hath taught me, I speak these things. . . . for I do always those things that please him" (John 8:28–29).

King Benjamin, an ancient prophet-king recorded in the Book of Mormon, understood the principles Jesus taught when he warned his people to watch themselves and their thoughts and their words and their deeds (Mosiah 4:30). He understood that the act of creation was lasting and had an impact on the spirits and lives of the creators. It is also interesting that he used the word "watch." This could mean to *be careful* what you think, speak, or do, but it also means *observe* your thoughts, words, and deeds. Observing my thoughts, words, and deeds allows me to understand what my feelings and emotions are behind the creation. I learn in what state my heart is, and it allows me to get closer to the source of those thoughts, words, and deeds.

I know that behind the words I speak and the thoughts that arise in my mind, there are emotions, feelings, energies, or vibrations. When I perform an act of service out of love, it feels beautiful and draws me closer to the recipient of that service. On the other hand, when I serve begrudgingly, I sense that the recipient can feel the lack of love. It is as if the creation itself has a memory of the emotion that was present at the time of creation. In Genesis chapter 1, we repeatedly read that after creation "God saw that it was good." There was obviously love attached to His creations.

I remember when I first started designing greeting cards, in order to make the card personal, I would think of someone that I loved and design the card for them, thinking of what they would love and what would make them happy. Just like I did when I was younger and designed cards for my family or friends. In other words, my *intention* while designing was to design it *for* someone I loved, the result was always fabulous, always a positive experience, and a design I was certainly pleased with. When I neglected to design with that intention, the design was a struggle and sometimes fell flat, or at least was not one that I was as happy with. I have found that even in the seemingly mundane things I do or think, I can choose the emotions through which I create. President Uchtdorf admonished us, "Because love is the great commandment, it ought to be at the *center* of all and everything we do . . . Love should be our walk and our talk."[4]

Do I create with underlying stress, contempt, insecurity, anger, or spite or do I choose to create with love, reverence, and joy?

So now I know that everything that I do becomes how I grow and blossom as a creative being. My life is my masterpiece. I am the creator. I am the designer. In every moment of my day—a kind word, a facial expression, or noticing a flower—I can ask myself, "what do I want to create?" I love how Ken Wilbur explains, "Your own basic awareness—and your very identity itself—is without boundaries."[5] When someone says they are not a creative person, they are putting a boundary on their identity, and there are no boundaries on their identity. So, are *you* a creative person? YES! Are you a wonderful being full of light? YES! Are you a healthy person? YES! Are you finding new ways to express your creativity? YES! We are all of those things and more, because there are no bounds to our identity except for those that we put on ourselves.

Marianne Williamson, author and teacher, said in her book, *The Law of Divine Compensation,* "Nothing binds you except your thoughts; nothing limits you except your fear; and nothing controls you except your beliefs."[6] Recognizing the truth of these statements makes the following statement from Elder Lawrence E. Corbridge even more significant. He said, "The challenge is not so much closing the gap between our actions and our beliefs; rather, the challenge is closing the gap between our beliefs and the truth. That is the challenge."[7]

---

4. Dieter F. Uchtdorf, "The Love of God," *Ensign*, November 2009.
5. Ken Wilbur, No Boundary (United States: Shambhala, 2001), viii.
6. Marianne Williamson, The Law of Divine Compensation (United States: HarperOne, 2012).
7. Lawrence E. Corbridge, "Stand Forever" [Brigham Young University fireside, January 22, 2019], speeches.byu.edu.

His point was that our actions naturally follow our beliefs. You can know my beliefs by watching my actions. Therefore, aligning my beliefs with truth is the most sure way that I can change my behavior.

The intention of this book is to allow *you*, the reader, to first come to an understanding of the truth that everything that happens in your life is an act of creation. Knowing this truth is the beginning but using this truth to change *what* you are creating is the key to designing your life in beautiful and meaningful ways. The seven principles outlined here are meant to assist you to put the intention and active participation back into the creative process that is happening moment by moment in your life. These principles are meant to be practiced as you read. You will come to see, as we have, how they amplify and strengthen the creative process.

We have also included a workbook to assist you in having experiences and creating your *own* practices that will incorporate and strengthen these principles into your creative process. Each moment of our lives has transformative power and anyone that chooses to apply these principles to the creative process in each moment of their lives will step into their God-given creative power.

Connection—Create purpose and meaning in connecting with myself, the Divine, and others.

Creativity—Exercise and strengthen my creative muscle daily to think outside the box in any part of my life.

Beauty—Learn how to create, see, feel, and build beauty in my life with courage and vision.

Play—Explore, rest, and relax my body, spirit, and mind with creative play.

Stories—My story sparks creativity and I see more meaning in my life.

Soul Work—Unlock authentic power as I create and hear my heart voice.

Abundance—Create "plenty" of time, energy, value, effort, ideas, and inspiration.

Principle 1 | CONNECTION

*I create purpose, meaning, and fulfillment in
connecting with my True Self, the Divine, and others.*

---

*"Connection is why we're here. We are hardwired
to connect with others, it's what gives purpose
and meaning to our lives."*

—Brené Brown[8]

THERE IS SOMETHING THAT HAPPENS IN LIFE THAT GIVES OUR LIVES such meaning and purpose and makes our lives rich and full. This something is connection. It fills the void of loneliness. It overcomes the feeling of pointlessness. It is why we are here, and it is one of the most powerful and treasured things we can experience. Without it, our progression is slowed, or reversed; we feel lost; we grow cynical and indignant; and we begin to believe that we are alone in the universe.

This is not the way God intended for us to live. He expects that we connect regularly to Him. He has organized us in family groups and created an innate desire for sociality to provide opportunities to connect with each other. And as part of our mortal experience, He has provided a mind that is self-reflective and gifted us with responsible choice that we may connect with our True Self.

---

8. Brené Brown, *Daring Greatly: How the Courage to Be Vulnerable Transforms the Way We Live, Love, Parent, and Lead* (United States: Penguin Publishing Group, 2012), 8.

Self Connection

I have had glimpses, over the course of my life, of my True Self. As a teenager, I remember someone saying something hurtful to me in junior high and feeling a voice of peace saying, "That's not true, that's not who you are." As I was serving as a missionary, we were teaching a young woman, and as I was sharing the plan of salvation, my mind expanded, and I saw a vision of my premortal self. It was another glimpse of who I really am. Another time, I was teaching a Sunday School class, and I was bearing my simple testimony of the things we were talking about (bearing testimony was one of my biggest fears as a young woman). I suddenly felt the wave of the Spirit wash over me, and I saw with spiritual eyes into the eternities and understood who I am, and that one of my spiritual gifts is to bear testimony of my Savior. These and many other "glimpses" almost always occurred when I was exercising a spiritual gift.

I have learned that my True Self is not remotely defined by my physical appearance. I am 4'10" in stature, but I do *not* feel "short"' My True Self does *not* feel small. When people remark, "Oh you're so short," or "You're so small," I am sometimes surprised and must remember that to their physical senses I *do* appear small. I don't think of myself as small. My spirit is so much bigger than my body.

On January 10, 2016, in a worldwide devotional for young adults, President Nelson issued a recommendation to "true millennials" to learn who they really are. He counseled,

> Ask your Heavenly Father in the name of Jesus Christ how He feels about you and your mission here on earth. If you ask with real intent, over time the Spirit will whisper the life-changing truth to you. Record those impressions, review them often, and follow through with exactness. I promise you that when you begin, to catch even a glimpse of how your Heavenly Father sees you and what He is counting on you to do for Him, your life will never be the same![9]

9. Russell M. Nelson, "Stand as True Millennials" [worldwide devotional for young adults, Brigham Young University—Hawaii, January 10, 2016], broadcast. lds.org.

I took that recommendation very seriously and I can testify of President Nelson's promise: my life hasn't been the same since. In Eliza R. Snow's talk, "An Elevation So High above the Ordinary," she said that "to become queens and priestesses we must be business women."[10] The first time I read that, I felt a surge of current flow through my body and I knew this was part of my purpose. The Spirit taught me that she spoke not of the world's definition of a businesswoman, but of God's definition of a businesswoman: a woman in the business of doing the Lord's work. The "glimpses" of my True Self have turned to sustained, intense gazes. It is clear to me now when I'm connected to my True Self and when I'm not.

Jeff's path to remembering his True Self was different from mine in many respects. This is how he would describe it:

> I too had seen glimpses of my True identity, but I had built up such a strong wall of protection—a "persona," as psychiatrist and psychoanalyst Carl Jung called it—that it had been many years since I had seen or felt even a glimmer of my True Self. Don't get me wrong, I had built up a persona that seemed solid, strong, and righteous enough. I was serving in a bishopric and working at Brigham Young University and, by all accounts, I was doing well, and successful. But my service to God had shrunk to only include my church service, which was feeling stale and duty driven. I felt, as Elder Anderson had described, like I was dancing but hearing no music. To return to "hearing" the music of the gospel, I started reading daily from the scriptures about the life of Christ. I also started reading *Jesus the Christ* by James E. Talmage. I felt that reading about His life and ministry would assist me to feel closer to my Savior, which would then assist me in feeling that joy of serving both inside and outside the Church, and bring back the joy of worship. I had continued this practice for about nine

10. Eliza R. Snow, "An Elevation So High above the Ordinary," in *At the Pulpit: 185 Years of Discourses by Latter-day Saint Women*, ed. Jennifer Reeder and Kate Holbrook (Salt Lake City: The Church Historian's Press, 2017), www.churchofjesuschrist.org/study/church-historians-press/at-the-pulpit/part-1/chapter-14?lang=eng.

months. I had finished Talmage's book and was finding other resources to study and keep the life of my Savior a center point of my pursuit of the word of God. But I still felt a "ceiling of fear" that was keeping me from becoming the Lord's servant that I knew in my heart I could be.

I remember praying one day and asking God to assist me in breaking through these fears. I then began to get frequent promptings to study certain things, and people were brought into my life that taught me how to meditate, how to quiet my mind and to find my center, and perhaps most importantly how to be honest with myself and the world. I began to have experiences that allowed me to begin to cast off the heavy shells of armor and disguises that I had so carefully built up over the years. As the walls came down, I felt myself opening up to the love that was freely available to me from God. I began to see that the reason I was having difficulty loving others, *or* feeling love from them, was that I had stopped feeling worthy of love. I had put myself below everyone around me and could not find reasons they could love me.

I remember a particular epiphany as I was meditating on something I had read. I realized that there was a voice in my head telling me that if I revealed too much of my True Self or if I allowed people to see past the shells of armor, they wouldn't like what they saw. But that wasn't the lie that was doing the greatest damage. The voice could have just as easily told me that people *would* like what they saw, and the damage the voice was doing would be just as great. The great *lie* was not in what the voice was saying, it was in what the voice was implying. The false implication was that it *mattered* whether people liked or didn't like what they saw when I allowed the True Self to be perceived. I was then able to internalize the truth, which is that it only matters to me and to God what my True Self is worth. And since God's love is unwavering and unconditional, and since I know that the worth of my soul or my True Self is infinite and absolute, I can live my True Self and break down those walls of protection every day, all day long, because what other people think of me, or how they see my value or worth has no bearing on how I see my own value or worth. As Kimberly Giles says in her book *Choosing Clarity,* "the only way to win this game is not to play."[11] I stopped playing the game and my life changed almost overnight. Of course, the work goes on. There are many old habits that continue to come up. Old triggers that recall the tendency to get back in the armor. But as I continue to use the tools I have gained, many of which we explain later in this and other chapters of this book, I step further into the light of the joys and beauty of life.

So, what is Self Connection and why is it such a big deal? Well, Self Connection is another way of saying being honest, being "present," and being "in the moment." It is using my consciousness in a way that allows me to be aware of my thoughts and feelings and what may be triggering them. It goes back to watching your thoughts, words, and deeds. In other words, don't lose track of what you are thinking and feeling and the sources of those thoughts and feelings. It is a state of being that puts you in a position to act rather than "be acted upon."

But beyond that, Self Connection is giving myself the opportunity to see and feel my True Self. For me, this means accepting the counsel of President Nelson to "ask your Heavenly Father in the name of Jesus Christ how He feels about you and your mission here on earth." Jeff's journey was similar in that it included a great deal of prayer and then he was led to the truth through his studying and through the assistance of wise people that were brought into his life. For both of us, the vision of our True Self became clearer as we worked to peel back the layers of fear and doubt and allow God to show us how He sees us.

Honesty is an essential part of Self Connection. Another meaning for honesty is "being one with what is." There are many ways that I can see when I am not honest with myself or true to myself. It might even be that I am so far from feeling or knowing what my True Self is that I don't know *how* to be honest with myself. That, to me, would feel like being totally lost.

---

11. Kimberly Giles, *Choosing Clarity: The Path to Fearlessness* (United States: Thomas Noble Books, 2014).

My True Self has messages and prompts for me. These prompts and feelings come through promptings from the Holy Ghost or from my own spirit, which is endowed with the Light of Christ, and so already knows, much of the time, what choices would serve me and others best. These prompts are the pure guidance that allow me to be who I am meant to be, to fulfill the measure of my creation and rise to my full spiritual stature.

Following the prompts can be a challenge, a stretch for my True Self, especially if I am being prompted to do something that I really don't believe I know how to do. But the point is not to do the thing perfectly, it is to listen and follow the prompt. As I listen and follow, I get better at doing the things I am prompted to do and the prompts from my Spirit, or the prompts from the Holy Ghost, come more frequently and with greater detail. The point is to stay true to myself by acting. This is the last part of President Nelson's counsel: "follow through with exactness."

What is my purpose?

There is an exercise where you keep asking yourself why you do the things you do, until you can feel that the answer is totally honest and at the very core of what you desire. When I did this exercise, I kept stopping before I got to the truth. When I finally got to the truth, I was surprised at how simple it sounded. The truth was that I was seeking peace and joy in my heart and mind, love for everyone and everything around me, and the ability to feel love flowing back to me. That was it. I wanted to give and feel love; feel happy and open all the time; 24–7. Now, that may sound selfish, but it's really just the opposite, because it involves acting toward other people and situations in a way that brings about or maximizes that feeling of love, joy, and peace. That can take a lot of effort in my heart, a lot of serving others, and a lot of quieting my mind.

The next part of the exercise is the hardest part, and it's done constantly over a lifetime. You go backwards and ask if the things that you're focusing on are in alignment with what you've realized you are truly seeking. While doing this exercise, if I find that they are not aligned with my true desires, I would ask myself if it is serving another purpose in my life that will increase the potential for feeling or giving love. Then I would get to decide if this was an opportunity to make a change in my priorities.

Jeff had a conversation with a good friend a while ago. He related this to me:

> This friend was worrying about some upcoming deadlines. He owns his own business and has a family that depends on the resources provided by that business. A big part of his job is looking at the future and trying to predict how things will play out so that he can manage the contractors that he has working on various projects. He called and laid out a major problem that was upcoming and that would affect his business in a very big way. He was very worried and was looking for solutions and assurances. I asked him if he was open for some coaching. He said, "That's why I'm calling you." I asked him to stop for a minute and ask himself why he was doing what he was doing. Obviously to make money and keep the business going. I asked "why" again. We went through this process to understand what his true underlying motivations were. In the end, the ultimate motivation was (and I'm paraphrasing here) that he would have peace and joy in his heart, time and a means to express his love for those closest to him, and to feel and give love and connect to all beings.
>
> Once the true motivations for all his work, focus, and energy were made apparent, the issue that was consuming him didn't seem that heavy. In fact, he admitted that the business would likely weather this storm, as it had done before. And he pointed out how he really *did* have the time, and the means, to do what he really wanted to do, which was be with his family and loved ones and enjoy his precious life. He felt like he was doing a pretty good job of that but could see how the business issue was distracting him from those supremely important pursuits.
>
> It's remarkable to me how easy it is to get distracted from what we truly seek. It is as if it gets buried beneath the very

methods we devise to obtain it. Perhaps this is why it seems so difficult to find our purpose. But the truth is, I don't find my purpose, I *create* it! Viktor E. Frankl, author, clinical psychologist, and concentration camp survivor, once said, "Ultimately, man should not ask what the meaning of his life is, but rather he must recognize that it is *he* who is asked."[12] God already knows what I'm going to create, so I can move forward with faith and trust. It is a law of heaven that I know intuitively in what areas I excel, or what my gifts and talents are. So, as I proceed through the process of creating, my purpose will become manifest because I will have created it. I take one step into the unknown and the Lord will illuminate that step. I choose to have faith in Jesus that what I'm doing *is* my purpose. Once I know this, it changes everything. This is not to say I won't go down a "wrong road" from time to time, but even that will never be a mistake as I get to take the lessons from that "wrong road."

As I create, it serves me to remember—I will always have a divine potential. Christ will always love me. I will always be a child of God. Christ knows my purpose and He makes all the difference.

God Connection

Connection to God is a spiritual connection. It is the free flow of love from God to me and from me to God. It is not only feeling His love—and knowing that I feel His love—but also feeling love for Him. All of God's children are entitled to feel His love and He loves us no matter what, but the connection occurs when the love is flowing both directions. In ancient times, King Benjamin, a prophet-king, spoke to his people about connecting with God: ". . . if ye have known of his goodness and have tasted of his love, and have received a remission of your sins, which causeth such exceedingly great joy in your souls . . ." (Mosiah 4:11)

---

12. Viktor E. Frankl, *Man's Search for Meaning* (United Kingdom: Beacon Press, 2006), 113.

The missing piece to the connection is often His children feeling love for Him. This prophet then instructed his people concerning that too. He reminds them of who God is and what He has done. He admonishes them to "remember, and always retain in remembrance, the greatness of God . . . and His goodness and long-suffering towards you . . ." He reminds them to humble themselves, call on His name, and stand steadfast in faith so that they would always be filled with the love of God (Mosiah 4:12–13). He gives the recipe for making the connection to God. First, recognize that He is the benevolent, loving Father that loves us no matter what. Knowing without a doubt that He loves me unconditionally and that He is a perfect God and His love is all encompassing, I am filled with gratitude. Then I not only increase my love for Him, but I open myself up to feel His love.

This connection to God assists me in so many ways. It is an infinite well of comfort in hard times. It gives meaning and purpose to suffering *and* to celebration. With my Divine connection, I feel my higher purpose. I awake everyday excited to live on purpose—live *in* purpose. This purpose gives meaning to everything I do in my day. Even in what some call the "mundane."

I had a hard time finding my meaning in the dirty diapers, the dishes, and the endless meals. But when I started making a habit of connecting to God in gratitude, there was no "mundane." There was a shift from "mundane" to *purpose*. Thanking God for the purpose of the dirty diapers, the dishes, and the endless meals, I choose to focus on gratitude. Gratitude for my children, my family, enough food, the joy of finding the Divine in the meals where we can gather, the accomplishment and fulfillment of these purposeful moments—working and laboring in love. This gratitude opens up my heart, mind, and soul; opening me to more gratitude, to more learning, to more love.

In the context of creativity, my connection to God allows me to know that there are things, moments, and situations in life that can be improved or served by Divine assistance. Having a connection with the Divine allows me to receive promptings, ideas, thoughts, feelings, or whatever it might be. Because I'm receiving it from the Divine source, I know it will serve me over time because I know God is love and this life is my perfect classroom. I create an advantage over the simple human strugglings, and through the connection, I know He consecrates my efforts for my good. I love this quote from Neal A. Maxwell:

> If you and I were left . . . to draw conclusions or generalizations from our small, personal databases, we would not be very wise. But we can access the divine database through the scriptures and prophetic utterances, acquiring perspective about 'things as they really are' (Jacob 4:13). Otherwise our generalizations won't be worth much more than the one I encountered years ago: 'All Indians walk single file, at least the one I saw did!'[13]

Making a connection with God is certainly a unique experience for every individual, but there are some key elements that Jeff and I have found as we have worked to keep that connection more permanent in our lives. One is gratitude. Gratitude and love are intertwined. Gratitude allows the free flow of love back and forth between me and God. Once I stop being grateful, I cut off the connection. This connective gratitude infuses our lives with love, meaning, and purpose. In many respects, gratitude IS the connection.

At a time when Jeff was struggling to feel God's love, which was showing up as his own difficulty extending love to others, he reestablished that deep personal connection by first thinking of the most loving person he could remember in his life. This mental exercise gave him a greater appreciation for all that God has done for him and for the love that he recognizes from Him. He related:

> I was in a place in my life where I guess I "felt" worthy to feel God's love, but my attitude was not in a good place. I was choosing to feel overburdened by responsibilities and others' perceived expectations of me. I couldn't figure out why I felt so annoyed and encumbered when I knew that I was supposed to be serving, giving, and loving. So I thought about the man that served as my mission President in the Philippines and how much I knew he loved me. I remember just being in his presence; the way he would greet me; how he spoke to me; how he would look at me. I remember feeling his love so

13. Neal A. Maxwell, "Brim with Joy" [Brigham Young University devotional, January 23, 1996], speeches.byu.edu.

strongly that if he had asked me to do anything, I would have done it for him, cheerfully. Then I realized that this was God's love. This man was channeling God's love. I began to imagine God connecting with me in the same way this beautiful man did. I imagined what God would say to me coming from that space of perfect love. I imagined Him asking me to serve, give, and love and it allowed me to change my attitude and view my responsibilities as opportunities to learn and grow and show my love for God.

I have found it easier to connect when I intentionally create a moment to *ask* to feel His love through prayer and meditation. I *seek* the connection by creating a mindset of gratitude and perspective of myself as a child of God, beloved by Him. This I do by experiencing His word or getting inside the temple. Then I *knock*. I act. I find a way to serve someone and open my heart in humility and let go of my distractions. And then, as He promises, I find—or feel—His love.

However, "ask, seek and knock" doesn't mean "sit and wait for it to happen." It's not a magical thing! I am expanding my vision of what it means to be a creator! It is up to me to make it happen; to *create* the connection. I *create* the connection to "Hear Him." I *create* the connection to access His atoning power. President Nelson has said,

> When you reach up for the Lord's power in your life with the same intensity that a drowning person has when grasping and gasping for air, power from Jesus Christ will be yours. When the Savior knows you truly want to reach up to Him—when He can feel that the greatest desire of your heart is to draw His power into your life—you will be led by the Holy Ghost to know exactly what you should do.[14]

There are practices that Jeff and I have that assist us in keeping the connection to God strong. It is hard not to try and find some unique magic bullet that no one has ever thought of, but the reality for both of us is that it was mostly practicing what we all have learned over and over again, but changing the quality . . . and the intensity. Here are a

---

14. Russell M. Nelson, "Drawing the Power of Jesus Christ into Our Lives," *Ensign*, May 2017.

few ideas that are merely our own spin on the tried and true methods for connecting to God:

Centering in the Spirit

I center in the Spirit by paying attention to how the Spirit talks to me. What does His language sound like; feel like? "The fruit of the Spirit is love, joy, peace, longsuffering, gentleness, goodness, faith, meekness, temperance [self-control]" (Galatians 5:22–23). I rather like the flow of *The Message* version of Galatians:

> But what happens when we live God's way? He brings gifts into our lives, much the same way fruit appears in an orchard—things like affection for others, exuberance about life, serenity. We develop a willingness to stick with things, a sense of compassion in the heart, and a conviction that a basic holiness permeates things and people. We find ourselves involved in loyal commitments, not needing to force our way in life, able to marshal and direct our energies wisely.[15]

I love the phrase, "a conviction that a basic holiness permeates things and people." It is such a great description of living life with reverence.

The Power of "I AM" statements

I am learning the power of creating my own "I AM" statements (*creating* here means not only to come up with them, but to speak them). The process of creating "I am" statements is personal and powerful. These statements allow me to manifest who I am and what I am creating. I create mighty truths in my declarations and in those declarations I feel closer to God, the Ultimate Creator, who declared that He exists to Moses, "I AM THAT I AM" (Exodus 3:14) or "I Am because I Am." "Behold, I am the Lord God Almighty, and Endless is my name" (Moses 1:3). We are eternal beings. We are the seeds of godhood. When we declare who we are, something resonates in our souls.

---

15. Galatians 5:22–23 (MSG).

Gratitude Practices

One of the gratitude practices that strengthens my connection to God is a process I used to overcome my false body image. It helped me see and feel my great worth in God's eyes and therefore allowed me to connect with Him in gratitude for a body I was fighting against most of my life. Gratitude and love are intertwined. When I meditate and go through each part of my body expressing LOVE for my eyes, nose, mouth, chin, jaw, etc, I *feel* the free flow of love back and forth between me and God.

Jeff's gratitude practices:

> There have been many times when I find myself in the midst of a difficult or stressful situation and I stop, regain my self-awareness (become fully present) and choose to say, "I'm glad I'm here learning this. I'm glad I have this life and get to learn and experience so many crazy things." Recognizing that, even in the hardest times, I can find my way to a perspective that there is something greater than this hard moment right now and that it is actually awesome that I get to have this experience. The experience is no longer the master. I get to master this experience with divine assistance from He who overcame all things, Jesus Christ. How I respond to the experiences determines whether I live in heaven or live in hell, now and in the eternities. The freedom to choose this response gives me great gratitude.

Prayer

When I pray, I love visualizing myself in God's presence. I recognize that I am connected to God through the covenants I've made with Him and He has made with me. I trust in this covenant connection and call on His name daily in prayer to connect to Him through my covenants. In my mind, I not only visualize I'm in His presence, but I look to my covenants and the temple in how I'm connected to Him. I find great power speaking prayers out loud, creating my experience—like Joseph—in mighty prayer in my wilderness.

I connect with God, through Jesus Christ, using visualization and the power of words coupled with fasting. This has been a monumental way to connect with God, Jesus, the Holy Ghost, and my ancestors. I've learned that through fasting and prayer there are specific blessings and miracles that I've come to expect. I go to God with President Nelson's words in my mind, "Expect and prepare to accomplish the impossible." I've learned that when faith and righteous desires that accompany fasting and prayer comes from deep deep down—from my very toes—I can actually *see* the miracles happening through Jesus Christ. Fasting and prayer . . . and more fasting, is my connection to the heavens.

Jeff's prayer practice:

> It has always been a conversation, but it has served me more recently to begin the prayer with something that puts me in a mode of humility. I also have incorporated meditation into my prayers, or rather, I have invited God into my meditation, which made it feel more like prayer. With no words, but keeping His presence and connection, I empty my mind and move consciousness to places it serves: my heart, my head, my hands. I practice expanding my consciousness and sending light and love to individuals to whom God prompts me to send. When I'm done with meditation, I work to connect with those people that day.

Fasting

For me, fasting was always a difficult law to obey. It tested all my strength and self-discipline. When I fasted, I usually concentrated on my weakness and headache, and would end my fast in a bad mood. Yup, I'm being vulnerable here. Fasting was not my strength. Or so I told myself.

But, God was reaching for me and wanted me to reach for Him in His Law of the Fast. Little by little, His Holy Spirit would tutor me in a personal way. He led me to the Jewish tradition of "Esther Fasts" and to study the book of Esther where she asks Mordacai and all the Jews to fast with her and her maidens for three days, seeking the miracles they sought in saving their people (Esther 4:16).

Stories of my ancestors found me and rested on my heart; stories of their three-day fasts when faced with insurmountable obstacles on the Mexican Frontier and the miraculous answers and guidance they received from the Lord.

Church and family history came alive as I read about Joseph Lee Robinson and his family's health crisis on their trek to the Salt Lake Valley. They fasted for three days for their daughter to be healed. Joseph witnessed that she was healed entirely.[16] I saw myself in these stories and, as I entered a time in my life where I desperately needed my God to perform mighty miracles, I took His reaching hand. I learned what fasting really means to me. It isn't about the lack of food or water. It is about God Connection; connecting to Him in a way that is void of the distractions of food and water and filled with His teachings, His light, and His love. Now fasting *is* a strength and a great power in my life.

Jeff's experience with a different kind of fasting:

In 2018, Rhonna chose to practice Lent. She asked me if I wanted to practice with her. Normally, I think I would have refused, but the Spirit nudged me to be open and say "Sure." I half-heartedly prayed to know what I could give up for Christ and with what I would replace it. Again, the Spirit nudged me to give up worldly music. Don't get me wrong. I wasn't listening to really raunchy music, just stuff on the radio. And I'm not about to pass judgement on anyone that listens to popular music, but I knew and the Spirit definitely knew that this would make a huge difference for me. So, for forty days I stopped listening to music that wasn't expanding my soul or assisting me to connect with God. I replaced it with hymns, "Christian" music (who knew some of this stuff is really good), and the spoken word. After the forty days ended, Rhonna asked me what I felt or learned from our practice of Lent. I'll never forget the feeling as a lump in my throat started to form

---

16. Hyrum L. Andrus and Helen Mae Andrus, *They Knew the Prophet* (Salt Lake City: Bookcraft, 1974), 164–165.

and my eyes started to water a little and I said, "I'll never go back." I still get choked up thinking about the tender mercy that came of Rhonna including me in her journey.

So, I started memorizing some hymns and songs that were uplifting and that had meaningful words and music, and I sing those songs as I drive or as I work around the house. Some are hymns, pop songs, even country songs. I find myself singing the songs that will serve me that day or that express what I'm feeling for my Heavenly Father in that moment. Music is one of my most powerful tools to connect to God.

Human Connection

It should not surprise us . . . that Heavenly Father brings about these intersectings and intertwinings of our lives. So often (after something is over) we will say, "little did I realize" or "I had no way of knowing" in referring to these intersectings. But why should we be surprised? Each of us has circles of friendships, and within those lie the portion of the human family whom God has given us to love, to serve, and to learn from.

—Neal A. Maxwell [17]

There is a pattern in life. Once I "come to myself," I desire to be reconciled to God, bringing to me great joy or comfort, which I then desire for everyone else. This pattern shows up in scripture with the prophets Abraham, Enos, Nephi, Moroni, Mormon, and Alma. When they came to themselves, they then connected with God. Then they naturally began to "pray for their brethren." This desire to connect with others through love is charity. And it is part of the two great commandments: love God and love your neighbor. I find that when I see my own humanity in another person, and it reflects back to me, I am in a better position to love someone in spite of imperfections; even love them *because* of their imperfections. I know that if I can love them in their imperfections, I can love myself. It reinforces the love of my True Self and God.

Of course, it is easiest to think of connecting with the people with whom you are closest and have the strongest relationships. But these relationships are the pattern we can follow with all of our relationships. How does it feel to be with those closest to you? Can you open up and be your True Self? Can you let your guard down? Share your thoughts? Be vulnerable? Can they reciprocate? If so, hang on to that relationship and then make more just like it. These types of relationships have free flowing love and energy between the participants and that allows them to flourish. There are many relationships, however, that are based on an exchange, *not* necessarily backed by love. One side wants something from you and, if the relationship is going to last, will give you something in exchange. This is an arrangement, and it is not necessarily bad, as long as the participants aren't oblivious to the fact that there *is* an arrangement and that this is *not* love.

The reason love is never described in scripture as "unconditional" is that there is no such thing as "conditional" love. Once there is a condition, it changes from love to a contract, an agreement, a promise, even a covenant or something else, but it is not love. Divine love or the love of God for man never dies, never diminishes, never goes away *no matter what*! Is God's love less powerful, less encompassing, or less perfect than a mother's love? *No!* We intuitively know love. We must learn the intricacies of a relationship or the terms of an agreement, partnership, or covenant. We must learn the details of laws and blessings, but love is simple. Love is felt in the heart.

We connect truly when coming from a place of love and vulnerability. I have to be open in order to love. If I'm not open and vulnerable, I'm putting something up. I'm putting up a wall or a disguise or a mask as part of my persona. Could we say that being vulnerable is being humble? Submissive? Teachable? We could at the very least say that being vulnerable is revealing the True Self, or "showing up" in truth.

What is the value of connection to my role as a creator? The value of connection is the free-flowing energy of love that takes the individuals to a higher plane of love that they can't achieve on their own. There is greater energy and love between two people than there is separately in the individuals. But there's something more. Connection is part of inspiration. That higher plane of energy taps into a great creative power. So, the vulnerability not only facilitates the connection but also opens me up to the greater creative power that comes from that connection. Which is a fancy way of saying: when I meet someone, I get ideas if I'm not showing up in fear and my motivation is love. In their book *Along the Path to Enlightenment,* David R. Hawkins and Scott Jeffrey explain, "Love is misunderstood to be an emotion; actually, it is a state of awareness, a way of being in the world, a way of seeing oneself and others. Love for God or nature or even one's pets opens the door to spiritual inspiration."[17]

I want to have these connections; because they make things happen. As creative beings we are meant to connect and create together. Think of councils, collaborations, masterminds, or think tanks. When they are done in love, it can be the most powerful creative experience that a group of people can have. And when connection to the Divine is included, they become revelatory experiences. Anyone who has experienced this knows exactly what this is like.

When Jeff and I make a connection with a new person or group of people in a seemingly random way, there is almost always the comment on how "random" that was. It is then that we get to "wake" our awareness and realize that God just brought us together for a reason. Neal A. Maxwell stated that,

> None of us ever fully utilizes the people-opportunities allocated to us within our circles of friendship. You and I may call these intersectings "coincidence." This word is understandable for mortals to use, but *coincidence* is not an appropriate word to describe the workings of an omniscient God. He does not do things by "coincidence" but instead by "divine design."[18]

Jeff has found that he will pray to know who to serve that day, he *will* receive promptings to do something or connect with someone. He says that as soon as the prompting comes, his mind starts arguing about why it's a bad idea, or a bad time, or wasn't a prompting in the

---

17. David R. Hawkins and Jeffery Scott, *Along the Path to Enlightenment* (United States: Hay House, 2011), 121.
18. Neal A. Maxwell, "Brim with Joy" [Brigham Young University devotional, January 23, 1996], speeches.byu.edu.

first place. He has found it is easier, rather than argue with himself, to tell the voice inside his head that it is probably correct, but that he's going to do it anyway. And then he heads for the door.

His connection with the Divine is key in knowing what to do or who to serve in acts of kindness and love. The trick, for him, is to do what He says when He says it. As the Holy Spirit—God's messenger—inspires him to serve and show kindness, he is opening up to human connection in a synergistic way. And then it just happens. It's a fruit of the Spirit; a fruit of love and charity that comes because of the connection with God and his True Self. We all have the power to raise each other up as we show kindness. Kindness is love. We all recognize what that looks like and feels like. Kindness has the power to break down barriers

Feeling God's love gives me permission to love myself. Feeling God's love for others gives me permission to love others. It's not a level or priority; it all is infused into the great commandment to love. We are all worthy of this love. We are made to love. It's a circular flow and flows in and through us from God and back. But we get to choose to create the connections. When everyone is connected to the True Self, to God, and then to each other, it is like there's a pillar of light to the group and to the Divine and back. And we call this the "Light Fountain." When you are making that connection with True Self, the Divine, and others, that is true love and light and energy. This is the energy of the universe.

Principle 2 | CREATIVITY

I exercise and strengthen my creative muscle daily to think outside the box in any part of my life.

You may believe that you are responsible for what you do, but not for what you think. The truth is that you are responsible for what you think, because it is only at this level that you can exercise choice. What you do comes from what you think.

—*A Course in Miracles*[19]

WHAT IS CREATIVITY? I THINK FOR MOST PEOPLE, CREATIVITY IS A certain quality or ability to transcend the norm or the conventional and come up with something that is original and new. But even when I am mimicking something, there is creation involved. I am creating something new for myself. If I say something that has already been said, it is not original, but it is a creation for me as I form the words. For our purposes here, we are going to expand the meaning of creativity to include the ability to participate in any and all acts of creation.

So, what is creation? Author and scientist Gary Zukav digs deep as he explains creation, "No form exists without consciousness. There is Light, and there is the shaping of Light by consciousness. This is creation."[20] While that statement may seem a bit philosophical, there is truth that we can all find in it. There is something special about

---

19. Helen Schucman and William Thetford, *A Course in Miracles* (United States: Ancient Wisdom Publications, 2008), 28.

20. Gary Zukav, *The Seat of the Soul* (United States: Simon & Schuster, 2007), 89.

light and there is definitely something special about my consciousness. Both are elements of creation. Creativity is light. Creativity is the *act* of giving form to light. A thought is creativity. The thought turning to a word or an action is an act of creativity. These are all raw materials that we use to make form.

In the creation narrative referred to throughout scripture, it is explained how "They, that is the gods" took unorganized matter and used it to *create* the heavens, the earth, and all things even mankind.[21] God's pattern for creation is an active process. He puts Himself into His creations. When I follow that pattern, I give form to raw material and I breathe life into whatever I create. Creativity is acting, not being acted upon.

Why is creativity important to me? As gods in training, we get to take that light and give it form. What does it do to my spirit when I act in creation? Creativity breathes life not only into whatever I create, but into me, the creator. I think of how I feel when I create something out of nothing. It allows me to "fill the measure of my creation." We all create. But *what* are we creating? Am I creating something that gives life to my family and surroundings or am I creating something that takes away from that life?

How do I create? It starts with a thought. Turning thoughts into words, actions. That is creating. We typically focus on creation as the fruits of the action, but it's really the whole process of creation—acting on a thought or creating words. But the key for me is to be intentional.

Jeff says, when he thinks of creativity, the hang-up he has is focusing on the mechanics of creating the work. The problem with that is that he can too easily say, "I don't know how to do that, I just don't know how to make that, or I am not a painter or a gourmet chef." He shuts himself down, focusing on the mechanics of creating the thing or the moment. He says, however, that if he will focus on what he intends to create, and the intention is very strong and very clear, he will just start the process and allow the mechanics to fall into place. He will pick up the guitar and start playing/practicing. He will learn the recipe as he does it. He can also change the intent from a completed product to the process itself. The intention can become, "I will

---

21. Genesis 1:1; 2:7; Abraham 3:24; 4:1; 5:7; Moses 2:2; 3:7.

enjoy the process of creating," rather than, "I will create an end product." He starts to see creation as a process and not just the fruit of that process.

For Jeff, this has also become how he views serving others. He says,

> If I focus on the mechanics, I will say, "I'm not going to serve this person because I won't know what to do or say, or it will be awkward." But, if I focus on the intention of loving my neighbor and showing him that love, the service becomes easier. And even though I may not get it right the first time, I get to let go of my expectations of perfection (or even expectations of proficiency) and allow the experience to teach me. My intention drives the mechanics and focusing on the intention is what assists me to see that I am becoming the best neighbor, best father, best son, or best friend.

"I am going to make the best meal I've ever made." There! I just said it. I began the creation by creating the words. You can call it "manifesting," "putting it out to the universe," or whatever serves you, but the point is you take the creative thought to the next level and then the next, and then the next . . . now I'm taking action. The alternative is the negative creation—allowing my circumstances to act upon me: "I don't have ingredients," "I've never done this before," or making the condemning declaration, "I don't know how to do that." I get to reverse and refine that process and I get to create.

> "Each word that you speak carries consciousness—more than that, carries intelligence—and, therefore, is an intention that shapes Light." —Gary Zukav[22]

How do I discover or develop creativity in myself? This is such a big question. And the answer looks different for everyone, but some general things that I feel will work universally: Be open and aware that creativity is happening all the time. Be present and in the moment, so that you can notice your creative process.

---

22. Gary Zukav, *The Seat of the Soul* (United States: Simon & Schuster, 2007), 108.

Developing Creativity

Jeff

I watch Rhonna go through her creativity exercises and then go to work. She is constantly creating. Some of it is incredible and some of it is . . . meh (by her own standards), but she does not stop. She is constantly discovering new ways to design images, fonts, whatever. She even creates while she experiences scripture. For her, her worship is a time to create and discover beauty. I adopted that in my journal writing. I pause from my dutybound push to record the events and write something fun, a poem, a funny story, or just nonsense, or I draw something to take my mind back to the creative process. I believe Rhonna has completely internalized what this quote from Jen Hatmaker is teaching:

> Say yes to that thing. Work with a mentor. Stop minimizing what you are good at and throw yourself into it with no apologies. Do you know who will do this for you? *No one. You are it.* Don't bury that talent, because the only thing fear yields is one dormant gift in a shallow grave. How many trot out that tired cliché—"I'm waiting for God to open a door"— and He is all, "I love you, but get going, pumpkin, because usually chasing the dream in your heart looks surprisingly like work. Don't just stand there, bust a move." (God often sounds like Young MC.) You are good at something for a reason. God designed you this way, on purpose.[23]

Rhonna

Most people acquainted with Jeff wouldn't know this about him (they will soon), but Jeff is an entertainer. He loves to entertain the kids and me. He is constantly making up stories in a foreign accent, sometimes he will go hours "in character" just to get the laughs. He will dance

---

23. Jen Hatmaker, *For the Love: Fighting for Grace in a World of Impossible Standards* (United States: Thomas Nelson, 2015), 33.

around the kitchen doing his "tip-top" dancing (a dance he made up as a spoof on "hip-hop"). He cooks (or experiments in the kitchen). Jeff sings. He loves to go out in nature. He can fix anything, or at least he will give it his best shot. He also uses creativity as a scientist. I know he is creative in the way that he designs experiments.

The two things that I *know* will diminish creativity: First, hoarding your ideas and creations, and second, doing nothing.

Strengthening our creativity comes in saying "yes!" "Yes" to being a Creator. "Yes" to being open and taking the opportunities to throw ourselves into what we create: thoughts, words, deeds/actions. This strengthens the creative muscle. And life has a way of presenting daily exercises, just like a workout program. If I'm feeling fear, that's the resistance. What I do with that resistance, becomes the exercise. Pushing through the fear, pain, or the hardship that is put upon me by others or life or myself, allows me to really become who I am to become.

I have these moments where I am not feeling fear, I am feeling love and beauty, and it might be fleeting, but those moments give me a view into who I truly am. Then something happens and the resistance is back. It's always coming up, but that can be good news too. Imagine you're a member of a sports team and your coach is a legend. She knows more about the sport than anyone else on the planet. She calls you into her office one day and says: "You could be the greatest member of the team. I see your potential and I also see what's keeping you from your potential. So, I've given you an exercise regimen to do daily. These workouts will strengthen where you are weak both physically and mentally. If you do these workouts faithfully, I can guarantee you will soon become the greatest member of the team." When you start doing the workouts, at first they are painful both physically and mentally, *because they are targeting where you are weak*. But in time these exercises become easier. And before you know it, you've achieved the goal that your coach set out for you.

An alternative ending to the story is that you refuse to do the exercises because they are "hard," so the coach demotes you to "second team" and eventually you leave the team in humiliation and bitterness. Then, perhaps over many years of struggle, you heal from this and learn the lessons that the coach offered for you to learn through her program of exercise and hard work. Those two paths are your choice. The coach in this story is God or life. God and life provide you with these exercises. I can choose to accept the exercises that have been given to me with wisdom and love or I can be forced to go through the humiliation and difficulty of the forced burdens. One is to choose to improve through wisdom and agency and the other is to choose to improve through forced circumstances and their difficult consequences. One is acting and one is being acted upon. When the coach calls you in and gives you the list of exercises, she presents you with a choice. "Either do the exercises and become who you were meant to become or don't do them and learn to become who you were meant to become a different way, *after* I kick you off the team." You will reach your potential regardless of the path you choose. The path will be different and your "potential" will look different too, but we are talking about spiritual potential, not physical.

This analogy may not resonate with everyone, but it points out a really surprising principle—a true principle. The coach (God or life) is offering the exercises to precisely target what will assist me to realize my highest potential, so I feel the resistance to breaking through to my potential. If the resistance isn't felt, it's not going to take me anywhere. So, in a way, I feel the resistance where I have great potential.

Another principle from the analogy is that the method of approaching the exercises is key. I can choose to focus on the weakness or failure as I attempt to do the exercises, or I can focus on the opportunity the exercises present to unleash my creative potential in strength. When the athlete goes into the weight room to workout, does she pick up the weight and just put it right back down and exclaim, "I can't do it, it's too heavy and I'm too weak"? If she does, she has literally missed the point of the exercise. She went into the weight room in the first place to provide herself with resistance. That is why she picked up the weight. I have learned that many addiction recovery programs teach the recovering addict that when they are tempted to return to their habit—and they *will* be tempted—the temptation is not an indication of weakness or failure. The temptation is the resistance. So, when they withstand the temptation, they are getting stronger, just as the athlete does when she lifts the weights.

The resistance, then, is *not* an indication that it's *not* working, but sometimes we look at our lives that way—when something is hard it is because we are not good enough, we are too weak, or a failure. But remember that the fact it's hard isn't an indication of failure, it's an indication of the resistance that life is offering so that you can get stronger. You *can* do it. You can create your strength. You can create beauty and meaning in your life. The exercise is what is creating the strength over time. The coach also knows that exercise will, in time, become more invigorating and more fun. Once the exercise becomes a part of who you are, it becomes natural.

God gives me exercises to perform on earth to become like Him. The exercises will be painful. I will feel the resistance, but they are specifically designed to tap that potential and unleash my superpower, which is: I am a divine child of God. I am a creator.

CREATIVITY EXERCISES: Thinking outside your box.

When I was in college, I had a professor who challenged us to pick five things that helped us feel creative. She taught us to do one of those things every day. And as we exercised our creativity, it would grow stronger and stronger. I took that challenge and grew with it. I added more creativity exercises to my list and felt my creative muscle get stronger. Over the years, I've honed these exercises and work out my creative muscle every single day. Now, this doesn't mean I get out my paints and brushes and create a canvas masterpiece every day. What it does mean is that I consistently do something that helps me feel creative. Whether it's a power nap, or an inspiration trip, or an exercise to look at things differently, these exercises kick up my creativity. They assist me in taking on the greater exercises that life presents to me. I have seen and felt my creativity surge by strengthening my creative muscle. I can honestly say I know I am a creator because I feel it.

How can I share my creativity? By contributing, creating even more, and achieving the joy in life I was created to feel. "Men [and women] are, that they might have joy" (2 Nephi 2:25). I can discover and unleash unlimited creativity as I share it with an open heart and an abundance mindset. I used to get all upset when another artist "copied" my work (or it was my perception that they were copying my work). But I came to realize that it didn't matter. Even *if* they really were copying me, the ideas are not mine alone. They come from the Source of all ideas and all creation. I get to now look to God with incredible gratitude as the source of ideas. It's just like love or money. When I hoard, I cut off the flow. The joy stops. Gratitude greases the skids for everything. It is the key to abundance in ideas, in work, in resources, in energy, and in creation. It unlocks the door to abundance, and it unlocks the door to positive energy and emotion. I love this quote that Gordon B. Hinkley said his father would use when someone was saying something negative: "Cynics do not contribute, skeptics do not create, doubters do not achieve."[24]

Some points that I consider as I create:

It's not my idea in the first place. God shares them with me (and not just me). And I can share them with others. Gratitude.

If I hoard, the ideas evaporate.

What good is an "idea" if I am not sharing the work it creates.

When I close myself off to sharing, I also close myself off to receiving.

Isaiah 50:11: "all ye that kindle a fire, that compass yourselves about with sparks: walk in the light of your fire, and in the sparks that ye have kindled."

"While ye have light, believe in the light, that ye may be the children of light" (John 12:36). I like to think about light. It's the key ingredient in my creativity. I get to receive light through the connections I make with self, God, and others. Once again, I'm creating a "Light Fountain." If I'm sharing light to make a true connection, then I'm also receiving light through that true connection. "The light which is in all things, which giveth life to all things, which is the law by which all things are governed, even the power of God who sitteth upon his throne" (Doctrine and Covenants 88:13). Connecting by sharing my creativity is not just giving of light, ideas, and creativity, it is allowing the light to flow freely to me and through me, and gratitude opens that door.

Jesus said, "I am the light of the world" (John 8:12). Everyone one of us has creativity because light is the source. "That was the true

---

24. Gordon B. Hinckley, "The Continuing Pursuit of Truth," *Ensign*, April 1968.

Light, which lighteth every man that cometh into the world" (John 1:9). *Light is powered by love.* So, if light is powered by love, connection is powered by love. Creativity is powered by love. In that love, we lean into abundance and intention and we create.

Principle 3 | BEAUTY

*I create, perceive, feel, and build beauty
in my life with courage and vision.*

---

*"A queen is wise. She has earned her serenity, not having
had it bestowed on her but having passed her tests. She has
suffered and grown more beautiful because of it. She has
proved she can hold her kingdom together. She has become
its vision. She cares deeply about something bigger
than herself. She rules with authentic power."*

—Marianne Williamson[25]

WHAT IS BEAUTY? A LIMITED DEFINITION OF BEAUTY IS SOMETHING
that invokes pleasure through or is pleasing to one of the five senses
or something that when experienced through the five senses produces
a positive emotion or feeling. What if we drop the "five senses" part
of that definition and expand it by saying that beauty is something
that when it is experienced it invokes pleasure to or lifts the heart
and spirit and produces a positive emotion or feeling? This feels more
accurate. There have certainly been moments in life when everything
hitting my physical senses would, under normal circumstances, have
produced very negative emotions or feelings, but in that moment, I
was able to perceive in the experience, something beautiful. Beauty,
then, is highly dependent on my perception.

---

25. Marianne Williamson, *A Woman's Worth* (United States: Random House
Publishing Group, 2013), 10.

If this is true then, as in the example above, there will be times in my life when my five senses are experiencing ugliness, but if I am open to it, my heart and spirit can perceive the beauty in the moment, beyond the five senses. If I'm not open to it, however, I can easily get distracted by what my five senses are experiencing and be blinded to the real beauty of life. Similarly, if my heart is full of fear or anger or bitterness, I can be blind to the beauty that is literally all around me, even what might be bombarding my physical senses.

Remember when Jeff encouraged me to make my dreams happen? Well, I dug deep and started the journey. Now, this was before the days of Google and Wiki-anything. The internet was just warming up, so I got to learn how to submit my artwork to greeting card companies the old-fashioned way—by snail-mailed portfolio. I would take our babies to the public library and scour the books with information for graphic artists. Through much prayer and seeking God's help, He led me to various books that gave me company profiles, their graphic design niche, and the names and addresses of those to contact. I started creating my portfolio when our babies were asleep. I worked my heart out and created samples of my work that I loved. I started to send my portfolio out to these companies and the rejections came back right away. Rejection after rejection. I wish I would have counted how many, but it seemed like hundreds at the time. Finally, one day, when I went to the mailbox and saw an envelope from a greeting card company, I told the Lord, "If this is another rejection, I'm done. I just can't keep doing this. I'll see it as a sign and know I need to pivot and do something else." It was a beautiful summer day in Minneapolis, Minnesota as I sat down in our backyard with our babies playing on the grass, and carefully opened that envelope. It was another rejection. I burst into tears right there on our back porch and sobbed. I was done. But in that moment, as our cute little girls were comforting me, I heard God whisper through His Holy Spirit, "Just keep going. Someone will love your art." And in that moment, I had a choice. I could listen to my hurt self and say, "Nope, I'm done." Or I could let His encouragement sink into my heart and follow His whisper. I chose to keep going. I chose to trust in Him and believe He had given me talents that would uplift and inspire others; that someone would like my art. He gave me vision and courage in that moment. And I clung onto it month after month. Not long after, the day came when I got my first acceptance letter and was soon designing my own greeting card line with a company who loved my art. God nudged me to go just a little farther and that nudge propelled me into a beautiful journey of uplifting and inspiring others with my creations.

There are so many things that happened that summer day in Minnesota that have taught me about beauty. I can now look back on that moment and see the beauty of the experience. I feel the love and encouragement from God, and I feel His loving push to keep going, to keep trying, and to learn what He knew I needed to learn. This is part of the beauty of that moment, but there was so much more. I was sitting under a giant oak tree on a beautiful summer day with my two beautiful little girls playing happily on the grass, but my mind was so full of fear and expectation, that I was blind to my surroundings and to the present experience. I wanted the acceptance so badly that I had taken myself out of the beauty of the moment, the beauty that was literally flooding my physical senses and could have been flooding my heart.

So much of what was beautiful in that moment had to do with my perception of what is beautiful. For me, life's not just about surrounding myself with beauty, it's about perceiving the things around me as beautiful. Which is a completely different thing. That doesn't mean that I don't work to make my surroundings beautiful. But as I expand my perceptions of what is beautiful, I begin to see that beauty is a mixture of what I can make beautiful with the gift of creativity God has given me, and what God has already made beautiful for me.

But as I look into my life, I may find hardship, tragedy, suffering, a dysfunctional family, or no family at all. How do I choose to find beauty where I don't see any? Something that has assisted me is to strive to "see" with spiritual eyes. Jean B. Bingham has taught, "Seeing with spiritual eyes enables us to develop an eternal perspective."[26] An eternal perspective is viewing my life as God sees it, and this allows me to see the greater purpose or meaning in those things I might describe as "hard" or even "ugly." Viktor E. Frankl—a man that saw a great deal of hardship and ugliness—wrote, "In some way, suffering ceases

---

26. Jean B. Bingham, "Catch the Vision, Share the Vision!" *Ensign,* August 2019.

to be suffering at the moment it finds a meaning."[27] If I can change my perception of trials, weaknesses, addiction, etc., they become my teachers and I get to thank God for the beautiful workout.

Finding some meaning or purpose to my hardships is the first step to finding the beauty in them. It takes courage and faith to perceive the beauty in the ugly, difficult, hard, or negative, and it may take years before I can look back and see the beauty in some experiences. But even remembering a difficult experience and intentionally seeking the meaning can assist me in knowing that there is meaning to my current hardships, even if it is difficult to see them in the moment. I can focus on the fact that they are providing the resistance that will make me stronger, or I can choose to view them as part of my "great classroom" experience. Creating beauty and meaning in my life is an everyday choice, an everyday design that I choose with courage, but I *can* choose to see every moment as beautiful because of the purpose and meaning it brings into my life.

If I can find beauty in memories of past experiences, then perceiving beauty definitely includes feelings and emotions. So, the heart, once again, has a great role to play in finding beauty. The scriptures are full of references to the heart finding the beauty of things. When a group of people in ancient America gathered in a location and came to a knowledge of the gospel of Jesus Christ and then made covenants with God, the waters there were described, "how beautiful are they to the eyes of them who there came to the knowledge of their Redeemer" (Mosiah 18:30). No doubt the location could have been physically beautiful, but the passage alludes to something deeper that was "seen" due to the experience of coming to a knowledge of their Redeemer. Many of us can think of someone that has come into our lives, that brought something of great value, like the gospel of Jesus Christ, or love, or purpose, or healing. Doesn't that person and your interactions with them become beautiful regardless of their appearance or the setting in which it occurred? From Isaiah we can read, "How beautiful upon the mountains are the feet of him that bringeth good tidings, that publisheth peace; that bringeth good tidings of good,

---

27. Viktor E. Frankl. *Man's Search for Meaning.* (United States: Beacon Press, 2006), 117.

that publisheth salvation; that saith unto Zion, Thy God reigneth" (Isaiah 52:7).

Perceiving and feeling beauty creates the positive emotions. Building beauty is altering my perceptions in order to live in those positive emotions. Isaiah continues in verse 9: "Break forth into joy, sing together, ye waste places . . . for the Lord hath comforted his people." I feel like rejoicing, singing, and dancing, and my life is filled with beauty, peace, and comfort through the Lord. He is beauty.

How can I rethink or rebuild my vision of beauty? In the book of Proverbs, we can read: "Where there is no vision, the people perish" (Proverbs 29:18). Experiencing life predominantly through my physical senses allows me to judge what is beautiful predominantly through those same senses. But, experiencing life through the heart and spirit includes my emotions, feelings, impressions, and intuition—all of my spiritual gifts—in seeking beauty. This allows me to perceive beauty even in something that may not appear beautiful to my physical senses.

In one of many instances when Isaiah described the Lord Jesus Christ in prophecy, he wrote, "he hath no form nor comeliness; and when we shall see him, there is no beauty that we should desire him" (Isaiah 53:2). When I read this I wonder, would I have followed Christ, or would I have been a persecutor? Why did his disciples follow Him? It wasn't because of His appearance, as Isaiah teaches us. But they perceived His divinity, His mission, and His ministry. They followed their hearts and perceived His beauty. So, my answer is, of course I would have followed Him! I am striving to follow Him now and I've never seen Him with my physical eyes, I've never sat in His physical presence and listened to His voice with my physical ears. Everything I do to follow Him now is done in faith. I perceive His beauty with my heart, as His disciples did so long ago.

So, I *can* rethink or rebuild my vision of beauty. I can pray for my heart to change. I can seek Christ's atoning power to be enabled to see with spiritual eyes—make that shift of perception—using my faith in Christ. Then acting in that, I put my trust in His enabling power and do all I can. I speak the change of heart, feel the change of heart, and act the change of heart like it's already happened. I manifest the beauty in my circumstance, watch the beauty come into my life, and then give thanks to God for Christ's miraculous works in my life.

How do I begin? One way to start is by finding the meaning in our circumstances. When life has meaning, it is beautiful. Viktor E. Frankl wrote, "I wish to stress that the true meaning of life is to be discovered in the world rather than within man or his own psyche." He further taught that there are three ways to create meaning in life (which always changes but never ceases): "(1) by creating a work or doing a deed; (2) by experiencing something or encountering someone; and (3) by the attitude we take toward unavoidable suffering."[28]

I have learned to create beauty in my life with my thoughts, words, and deeds. Referring back to creation, I can create beauty through powerful words, beautiful thoughts, and kind deeds. And when they are in alignment with my definition of beauty—once I know what beauty is to me—then they are in alignment with the deeper meaning and purpose of the world around me. Again, I take the counsel from the ancient prophet, King Benjamin, to watch my thoughts, watch my words and watch my deeds. I can choose my thoughts, words, and deeds to create the meaning—to create the beauty. When my thoughts, words, and deeds are assisting a connection with love or assisting to create beauty, and if they are uplifting, inspiring, and moving me towards my goals and moving others toward their goals—this is meaning and this is beauty.

Practices

Work to use the positive way to speak. Work on saying the good things that you will do; not the bad things that you will stop doing. Speech is powerful and saying what you won't do is not creating meaning; it's not pushing you towards where you want to go. It's making present the place you don't want to go. Check your words. Do they expand the soul with light and love or do they contract and shrivel the soul? Just practice this and see the beauty and meaning come to fruition in your life.

What can I do when I still can't see beauty in my circumstance? The process of just looking for beauty outside of myself will show

---

28. Viktor E. Frankl, *Man's Search for Meaning* (United States: Beacon Press, 2006), 115.

me the things I care about. Viktor E. Frankl says, "The second way of finding a meaning in life is by experiencing something-such as goodness, truth and beauty—by experiencing nature and culture or, last but not least, by experiencing another human being in his very uniqueness—by loving him."[29]

Finding the beauty within yourself helps you find the beauty outside yourself. In the Introduction, I told the story of how thinking of someone I loved while creating greeting cards assisted me in creating something that was far more beautiful than if I wasn't thinking of anyone to give the card to. As part of creativity exercises, we encourage you to think of someone you are creating for or think of why you are doing it. Then create. Love, meaning, and purpose strengthens the creative process and establishes a deeper beauty. Matthew 16:25 states, "whosoever will lose his life for my sake shall find it." We lose ourselves in the serving of others. And then the beauty inside ourselves is made manifest.

As our perceptions have changed toward beauty, our hearts open to love—it's as if our lives are illuminated. The sky is bluer. The trees are greener. The light is brighter. The "Light Fountain" is a beauty light. And when you turn it on in that "Connection sweet spot," then you can't help but to see beauty and meaning in that light. Beauty is illuminated.

---

29. Viktor E. Frankl, *Man's Search for Meaning* (United States: Beacon Press, 2006), 115.

Principle 4 | PLAY

I step into the creative process to explore,
rest, and refresh my body, spirit, and mind
with physical, mental, and creative play.

"Where there is a lack of rest, there
is an abundance of stress."

—Lysa TerKeurst[30]

PLAY BUILDS UPON AND IS A PART OF EXERCISING MY CREATIVITY, BUT it goes beyond that. For me, play is an enjoyable activity or experience without the expectation of a finished product. It includes rest, enjoyment, and sometimes just simple fun. That doesn't mean, however, that play can't be productive, but it's in the enjoyment and expectation (or lack of) that I find the meaning of play. If the expectation of a finished product is too high, then it's no longer play for me, it's an assignment or a project. By letting go of the expectation of an end product, it allows me to relax and explore new ideas that may or may not be fruitful, which can be a very exciting part of play.

Play has the ability to refresh the mind, body, and spirit. I think of it like a massage for my creative muscle. Physical massage brings blood to the muscles to nourish and heal them and get new life back. Creative massage, or play, is the same. It can renew my creativity and

---

30. Lysa TerKeurst, *Unglued: Making Wise Choices in the Midst of Raw Emotions* (United States: Zondervan, 2012).

bring the life back into my creation. As Brené Brown preaches, "Ask what makes you come alive, and go do it. Because what the world needs is people who have come alive."[31]

Jeff's refreshing play is canyoneering and rock climbing. This play brings risk, which he finds exhilarating. He says that mitigating the risks on these adventures is also part of the fun. Many times he has come back from a rock climbing trip or a canyoneering trip so excited about the events of the trip he can't suppress the permanent grin. And he will admit that he feels more alive.

Fun is a big part of play. What is fun? Enjoyment for the sake of enjoyment? Doing things for the fun of it? I'll doodle, create my own coloring pages, and color for the fun of it. I'll go for a hike or a walk, take a drive on a mountain road, gather with family or friends or tell stories. These are times that I give my mind permission to relax and *not* concentrate on being productive. That is not to say that play is necessarily an "escape," but it takes me out of my normal thought processes and routines and can even be a way to practice thinking outside myself. Many times some of my best inspiration comes from these "down" times. It's as though getting outside my daily routine sharpens my mind.

Rest is also a big part of play. It turns out that rest is built into many productive activities. Rest is found in farming. One season you don't grow anything in a field and it actually allows it to nourish the seeds more effectively in the next season. Our bodies grow in rest times. Through use and exertion, our muscles develop tiny tears. The rest gives them a chance to repair and grow stronger. Even distance runners have a theory about their running shoes. Buy two pairs of shoes and alternate running in them to give them a chance to "rest" so the padding lasts longer and replenishes better between use. I don't know the data on that last example, but I think we get the point. Our brain and body are the same way. Daily grind can wear them down. Rest is good and it can give the resting body a chance to get stronger.

31. Brené Brown, *The Gifts of Imperfection: Let Go of Who You Think You're Supposed to Be and Embrace Who You Are* (United States: Hazelden Publishing, 2010), 115.

In an article titled "Human Play and Animal Play—Why We're More Similar Than You Think,"[32] Dr Stuart Brown, a play researcher, reports that studies of play have produced a few concrete facts about play, namely:

- It is voluntary, people want to play and do it of their own accord.
- It appears purposeless—but really isn't. While time at play doesn't appear to fulfill any immediate life need (like eating or defending territory), it bestows many benefits long term.
- It can be interrupted (it is not compulsively driven).
- It is fun, pleasurable, and makes the player want to continue it.
- It is engaging and takes the player out of the sense of time.
- It really is a separate "state of being," and most of us recognize when an animal is full of play, or when we ourselves are experiencing it.
- It does not occur if the player is fearful, sick, or otherwise threatened.
- All animals that play, engage in body play. Movement alone can be joyous.

Children seem to have an innate desire and drive to play, and they will draw other children and adults into their play. As adults we sometimes suppress this desire or drive. We feel too busy or that it is no longer age appropriate to engage in play. As a young mother I started to feel like busyness was a badge of honor, that resting and relaxing were indulgent, and that play was wasting time or ineffective. (Now this would be a very puzzling statement for people that knew me in college where I would find any excuse to get out of studying and working.) While in Minnesota, with Jeff in graduate school, I was taking care of our two little girls and managing our household. Our oldest was three years old at the time, and I felt so busy. There was laundry to be done, shopping and making meals, caring for two small kids, keeping the old house we lived in clean and in livable repair. One

---

32. Stuart Brown, "Human Play and Animal Play and Why We're More Similar Than You Think," *National Institute for Play*, December 7, 2017, https://www.playcore.com/news/human-play-and-animal-play-why-were-more-similar-than-you-might-think.

day as I was busily taking care of my checklist, our oldest looked up at me and said something like, "Mom, it's time for you to come and play." She was trying to say, why don't you get down here and play with us? I thought, "Oh my goodness, I've let myself get so busy running on this hamster wheel that I won't jump off and sit down with my girls and play with them." It was a much-needed course correction, and it wouldn't be the last.

Dieter F. Uchtdorf taught,

> Let's be honest; it's rather easy to be busy. We all can think up a list of tasks that will overwhelm our schedules. Some might even think that their self-worth depends on the length of their to-do list. They flood the open spaces in their time with lists of meetings and minutia—even during times of stress and fatigue. Because they unnecessarily complicate their lives, they often feel increased frustration, diminished joy, and too little sense of meaning in their lives.
>
> It is said that any virtue when taken to an extreme can become a vice. Overscheduling our days would certainly qualify for this. There comes a point where milestones can become millstones and ambitions, albatrosses around our necks.[33]

As our family was growing, we reserved Monday night as the night that our family would do something together. As part of that night, we would spend a couple of minutes to go over our schedules, talk about family business, and plan out the week. As our children got older and more involved in things, I felt this part of our evening became increasingly important to keep us from double-booking and to make sure everyone knew when and where they needed to be. But because of this, "busyness-is-good" mindset that I was in, I would always start this part of our evening like I was ramping up for battle. I'd take a deep breath and say something like, "Ok, this is gonna be a crazy week!" or "Ok, we've got *a lot* going on this week!" One night, after I made this announcement, Jeff said to me, "Why do you do that? Why do you make it sound like every week is going to be horrible and stressful? We haven't even started to be busy and I'm already

---

33. Dieter F. Uchtdorf, "Of Things that Matter Most," *Ensign*, November 2010.

stressed out about our week." His comment gave me a chance to stop and reflect on why I was facing my week like that. I realized that if my focus had been on all the fun things we could do that week, I might have started by saying, "Ok, this is going to be the best, most fun, most enjoyable week of our lives! Can I get an 'amen'?"

This was a paradigm shift for me. It wasn't that I didn't know how to play. I had already incorporated play into my creativity exercises and made it a priority for our family and me, but I wasn't seeing it as part of our weekly schedule. All I could see were the things that made my week look busy, hard, overloaded and "crazy," and that was how I was describing them. I thought that's just what you did. I wasn't allowing the play to have its desired effect in *all* parts of my life. I remember thinking, after Jeff's comment, "Wait, I have choice? I don't have to look at this in a way that feels overwhelming or makes me feel like I'm gonna go crazy?"

I got to change the way I perceived and talked about my week. I made play intentional and gave myself permission to view play as an essential part of my schedule and look at my week as a combination of work *and* play. I changed how I announced our week and that changed the feeling for the whole family. The work that was ahead of us also started to look enjoyable. I felt like I had been freed from a mindset and therefore freed from the feeling of busyness.

Jeff, my favorite scientist, has shared what he's learned about play:

> There is not a perfect answer for why we tend to stop playing as adults, and it would appear that we are actually designed to continue play throughout our lives. Researchers have noted that in other species the physical characteristics of the adult change dramatically to adapt specifically to survival functions such as hunting or obtaining food or defending territory or family. The brains of these species are also far less able to change, grow, and adapt in adulthood. However, in humans, perhaps more than any other species, adults retain many juvenile physical characteristics, and our brains retain their plasticity (ability to adapt, change, and replenish).[34] All of

---

34. S.J. Gould, "A Biological Homage to Mickey Mouse," *Ecotone*, January 2008; and Ashley Montagu, *Growing Young* (United States: Bergin & Garvey, 1989).

this indicates that we, as humans, are basically designed to continue to play throughout our entire lives. But as we will discuss further down, we are not only designed *to* play, we are also designed *by* play.

What role does play take in the creative process? It refreshes the mind, body, and spirit, and it allows us—depending on the activity—to explore things that productivity does not. Hiking on a trail, playing dress up, having a dance party, making yogurt, playing basketball with friends, doodling, singing in the car—it recharges your batteries. Makes you come alive. It can bring in and restore joy! Family trips and vacations don't just create memories and connections, but also allow the mind to explore new surroundings and see things that I'm not used to seeing, stimulating my mind and my heart, and getting me excited to create. If you're getting tired of the routine and you're not hearing the music anymore, play can assist you to hear the music and remind you *why* you are designing your life.

What's more, our brains are continually growing and creating new neural connections throughout our lives. Play assists the brain to create these new connections and then test them in a safe, non-essential activity (meaning not essential to survival). If the play that I choose to engage in is similar to my work as a designer/artist (i.e. coloring pages, doodling, hand lettering), it can strengthen and test current brain function, and when my choice of play is different, it can assist my brain to build new connections that may also get used in my creative journey. But now, I have expanded my abilities and my perceptions. I have created neural connections that may assist me to think and create a little differently. I have expanded my creative toolbox.

Play also has a role in connection. Have you ever watched a person interact with an infant child and wondered, "Why do they behave that way?" But then when it is your turn to hold the baby, you end up doing the very same silly voice and funny faces. This is a form of play at its most basic, and it is a form of connection between you and the infant. Dr. Allan Schore calls this attachment between a primary caregiver and an infant: attunement, and it is very strong and very important to a child's development. It also explains how a primary caregiver that frequently engages the infant child in this form of play can know the state of the infant child, and literally feel their emotions. But the attachment is also created, to a lesser degree with anyone that plays, in this way, with the infant. The brain activity of the players actually starts to sync.[35]

And this goes beyond playing with a baby. The same brain centers that are tuning in when playing with a baby are tuning in when playing a game with an adult friend, playing fetch with a dog, or pulling the yarn ball away from a kitten. According to Dr. Schore, "This mechanism occurs most prominently at later points of shared, spontaneous, improvised, and emotionally rewarding moments of intimate contact, including intersubjective play."[36] In plainer language this means that we can connect with each other through play.

I know that was all "science-y," but it's so powerful, we had to include it. It actually makes play "legit," right?

Play is also a precursor to Soul Work. It's a step toward meditation and other practices that give my mind a break from the constant flow of ideas, the chatter and the stress. Allowing myself to play, giving myself permission to rest, energizes me in a way that helps me be a creator of something beautiful and meaningful, not just productive. It increases my clarity, helps me prioritize, focus, and enjoy work. Before I learned to meditate, play was the best way I knew to give myself a break from the constant pressure to be productive and meet deadlines. Lack of play and lack of rest leads to stress in my life and a feeling of emptiness.

Play often reminds me why I work, or why I love to work. The saying goes, "Do you live to work or do you work to live?" Play reminds me why I like to be productive, and it's not so that I can make more

---

35. Vera R.R. Ramires, "The Intersubjective Nature of Play Development and Its Role in Child Psychoanalytic Psychotherapy," *Frontiers in Psychology*, November 15, 2016.
36. Allan N. Schore, "Playing on the Right Side of the Brain," *American Journal of Play*, Winter 2017.

money to play more! Play doesn't require money. No, play can get me excited for the things that I love to do, by changing things up and allowing me to enjoy the simplicity of creation. I often design my play around activities that apply to or are similar to the things I spend my time doing for "work;" choosing to play in a way that brings out the things I love. For example, when I color my own coloring pages, it reminds me why I love art . . . without deadlines. Writing my favorite quotes freestyle reminds me why I love hand lettering (and why I love the power of words). Jeff loves to "experiment" in the kitchen, but his "experiments" always have some element of science. Of course they do! He's a scientist at heart. The relatively simple science that he enjoys in the kitchen—fermentation, curing, smoking, getting temperatures just perfect—these all remind him why he loves to go to work and do research on relatively complex projects. And this explorative play can bring beauty and meaning in our lives without necessarily producing a finished product.

How do you play? Seems kinda funny explaining in a book how to play. One might think we are truly hopeless if we need that kind of instruction, but we're also talking about play as it relates to creativity. So of course, I can find any activity that brings rest and refreshment to my spirit, body, and mind and then make time to do it. *But* I can also find things that bring the enjoyment back into a hobby, an occupation, or get me started in something that has always interested me. Jeff started learning to play the guitar after 35 years of not touching one. He did it for fun and he says it is relaxing just to sit and strum and sing a simple little song or just hum it. Is there something that would assist you to relax if there was no pressure to produce, perform, or present? Dieter F. Uchtdorf said, "There is a beauty and clarity that comes from simplicity that we sometimes do not appreciate in our thirst for intricate solutions."[37]

Physical exercise can certainly be play. In young children we can clearly see how movement is an important aspect of play. They are still learning how to control their bodies, but ageing doesn't change the importance of this type of play. Our play researcher Dr. Brown pointed out,

---

37. Dieter F. Uchtdorf, "Of Things that Matter Most," *Ensign*, November 2010.

Learning about self-movement creates a structure for an individual's knowledge of the world—it is a way of *knowing*. Through movement play, we *think* in motion. Movement structures our knowledge of the world, space, time, and our relationship to others. . . . Movement play lights up the brain and fosters learning, innovation, flexibility, adaptability, and resilience.[38]

Sports (maybe not to the extent of unhealthy competition), getting out in nature, hiking, bike riding, dancing, and boating are types of play that allow us to move and access those benefits just listed. I may have outgrown turning a simple card game into a contact sport (Jeff contests that), but none of us have outgrown the desire, or need, for movement play. It offers an opportunity to connect in a fun, low-pressure way. We can foster stronger and more meaningful relationships by doing things together in the form of play.

As I step into different forms of creative play, I've found great strength in learning from God's patterns on how He creates. It is recorded as part of the creation narrative that God rested at the end of the creative period. "And I, God, blessed the seventh day, and sanctified it; because that in it I had rested from all my work which I, God, had created and made" (Moses 3:3; Genesis 2:2–3). Did the blessing and sanctification of the seventh day give greater reverence to His creations? Can I give greater reverence for the things I create with my God-given talents and gifts by creating a time and space to rest from my labors? I believe so, and I believe God has given us a pattern to follow.

The rest and restorative power of play allows me to recharge and then reconnect to those around me. It clears my mind and assists me to be present so that I can see with greater clarity who I am and what I am here to do. Because of this, the "Light Fountain" becomes more beautiful and full of joy as I step, more refreshed, into my role as the creator of my life and connect with the True Self, the Divine, and others.

---

38. Stuart Brown, M.D. and Christopher Vaughan, *Play: How it Shapes the Brain, Opens the Imagination, and Invigorates the Soul* (United States: Penguin Publishing Group, 2009).

Principle 5 | STORIES

I know who I am, and I build meaning and spark beauty into the stories of my life.

STORIES ARE OUR STREAMING, NARRATIVE CREATION OF THE EXPERIENCES of the past, and they are more powerful than many of us realize. They are magical, more than mere information. Stories have color and emotion. Even simple anecdotes can convey deep meaning. There are few people that don't like a good story, but if we think the magic of a story is only in its ability to allow the listener to temporarily escape reality, then I feel that we have missed the true power of a story.

Stories aren't just found in books and movies. Pictures, songs, our very lives are made up of stories. My dear friend, Allison Kimball, taught me that our spirits are made up of stories, so my stories started long ago and will continue into the eternities. The stories of my mortal journey not only add to my life, but they add to those that make up my spirit. I am continually creating more of my spirit through more of my stories, and I get to reflect, "What am I creating? What am I designing through my stories?"

---

39. Robert McKee, *Story: Substance, Structure, Style, and the Principles of Screenwriting* (United Kingdom: Methuen, 1999).

Telling and listening to stories are a discovery process, a process of learning and healing for both the listener and the storyteller. When I tell a story for a specific purpose, for example, with a purpose to heal, or to show forgiveness, or to teach a principle, it's what I call "intentional storytelling." It's telling a story to illustrate what our family does in certain situations, or what *I* do in those situations. I can learn who I am and assist others to learn their identity as I listen, share, and connect with my stories and others' stories. There are stories that I have told our children when they were young that, I now realize, assisted them in recognizing and strengthening their identities. The story doesn't become their identity. It doesn't even modify their identity. Rather, it becomes a story that they adopt to connect with their True Self. The right stories can open up the possibility for a choice to be made or a change to occur in a life. It gives the listener a new potential.

Jeff has a sister, Michelle, that was killed in a car accident when she was 21 years old and Jeff was 22. The two of them were very close and our kids never had the opportunity to meet her, so as they got older, we started telling them stories of Michelle. She is truly an amazing person. She's compassionate, mischievous, loving, and outgoing. Jeff says there wasn't a person in her high school that didn't know who she was and that didn't like her. She had a group of friends that she would do things with; sometimes they were testing the limits of what they could get away with and sometimes they really did some amazing things to serve other people. So many of her stories are full of funny events or harmless trouble she would get into, but some of them reveal her amazing courage, determination, and unfailing kindness. One of our favorite stories is that Michelle was always annoyed that she was the only one of Jeff's siblings that didn't have a middle name. So, when she was graduating from high school, the name she had the administration put on her diploma had a middle name (of her choosing). That story is almost too perfect to describe what Michelle was like. When we told these stories about Michelle to our kids, they resonated. It opened up possibilities. We began to see different behaviors that reflected some of the characteristics that came out in the stories. Our kids weren't becoming different people, they were opening up to new possibilities. It's as though the stories were giving permission for a part of their True Self to be realized. Is this why young children want to hear stories? Because they are hungry to discover who they are? The story does not create their identity, it gives them permission or perhaps courage to open up parts of their identity that maybe had been shut down, hidden, untested, or unknown.

As I was growing up, my dad would tell me stories about "Grandpa Gonzales" (this was my great grandpa Gonzales). He would tell us about how he had a gift for teaching and speaking; that when he taught, people would listen because he taught and spoke with "ánimo." He told us it meant something like with "fire" or passion, but I learned what "with ánimo" looked like by watching my dad teach. He had it too. Of course, speaking and teaching in front of people scared me to death, so the stories didn't resonate with me at first, but they stayed with me. And when I started teaching the gospel of Jesus Christ in Japan as a young woman, I finally felt what he meant by "ánimo." I could feel it in myself as I taught and, because of the stories, I knew it was part of who I am. The stories connected me to that part of my True Self and enabled me to choose to step into the power of that heritage.

Some stories will resonate, and some will not. Those that *do* resonate, I might adopt as part of the way I identify with my True Self. I remember reading a line from M. Catherine Thomas's *The God Seed*. She was telling of God and other "highly developed beings" and wrote that, "They developed unshakable confidence in Goodness and Truth as the way to do life. They practiced until they actually became one with these godly characteristics."[40] Their stories are of the "practicing" which contributed to their progression and growth. If the story is clothed in beauty and meaning, then the choice or possibility that it opens up can also appear beautiful and meaningful. If the story that opens a child to part of their True Self is told in a positive way from a position of love and acceptance, the part of their True Self that it opens up can be seen in that same light. *This is the power of stories!*

I can rediscover my past and see things from a different perspective as I share the joint narratives with family and friends through *intentional storytelling.* Since stories are the interpretation of past

---

40. M. Catherine Thomas, *The God Seed: Probing the Mystery of Spiritual Development* (United States: Digital Legend, 2014).

experiences through my present lens, this means that the story may be different now from how I perceived it at the time it happened. Seeing the experience from a different perspective can change how I prepare for the future and live in the present. We all know someone that repeats stories. I certainly do it. It's as though the retelling reminds me of the experience. It's a reliving of the experience that gives me an opportunity to reflect on the lessons of the story and learn something more every time I retell it. It can provide a chance to feel the emotions of the experience—the joy, sadness, or whatever emotion the story brings out—and let it go, if that is what serves me.

When Jeff was a teenager and going through some rough times—or maybe it was his parents that were going through the rough times—Anyway, he recalls his grandfather, Papa Reed, calling him up and asking him to go with him for a drive in this beautiful canyon just east of the town where they lived. Jeff agreed and they went for a drive. During the whole drive, Papa Reed was talking to him, telling him stories, asking him questions, not really offering any advice, just talking. At the end of the drive, Jeff said he was kind of confused, there was never any lecture or any counsel given, just talk. When Jeff told himself or his friends that story as a teenager, he probably would just scratch his head and say, "That was weird." As he got older, he would tell the story that his mother, in exasperation, probably asked Papa Reed to talk to him and see if he could "talk some sense into him," but that Papa Reed probably didn't know what to say, so he just talked and told stories. Now Jeff tells the story differently. He can see the situation with greater clarity and perspective. He sees that his grandfather knew exactly what was going on and knew just what to say to assist Jeff in feeling accepted and loved. His grandfather gave him an assurance that he believed in him, even if the situation didn't look so good or Jeff was not making the best choices at the time. And even though he didn't fully understand the "why" of this little drive with his Papa Reed, Jeff felt the intention and it had its effect. He weeps now when he tells the story. It has become one of the most endearing moments in his memory of his grandfather, because he knows without a doubt that his grandfather loved him without judgement and without reservation.

Some may say that we can't pick and choose our stories, and while I agree that we don't get to fabricate our history, we can, and do, share stories depending on what we want to create in that moment. Whether I want to create a moment of joy, forgiveness, healing, or connection, knowing what I want to create in that moment will assist me in selecting which story to tell. There were, and still are, plenty of times when the mood is light and our family wants to connect through stories of Jeff's or my childhood, funny things that happened or mischief we may have created at their age—our kids would ask us to hear our "trouble stories"—but there are also those times when someone is going through a crisis and a story of strength or faith is called upon. In those moments, the right story can act as a healing balm. It can provide just the right answers to just the right questions. They may not provide the solution to the problem, but they can answer the question, "Do I have the strength or the capacity to solve or endure this crisis?" and "Do I have to do it alone?" I love this thought from Morgan Harper Nichols: "Tell the story of the mountain you climbed. Your words could become a page in someone else's survival guide."[41]

When the crisis involves myself or a member of my family, I have found it very powerful to draw upon a story of one of my ancestors. Stories of my ancestors seem to have a different effect than those of my own life. Our stories are still being written. We are in the middle of moments filled with conflict, trials, love, joy, and growing. The stories of my ancestors have a beginning and an end. I can see their lives like looking through a book with transparent pages. It makes it easy for me and my family to see that their lives had great meaning and purpose. We can see their strengths and how they overcame great obstacles and tribulation. All of these things can be harder to see in my own story, but as I connect more and more with my ancestors, through learning and sharing their stories, I begin to see the same themes in my own life—the same strengths, the same purpose, the same resilience.

---

41. Morgan Harper Nichols, "Tell the story of the mountains you climbed. Your words could become a page in someone else's survival guide," Tumblr, May 19, 2018, https://morganharpernichols.tumblr.com/post/174058316843/tell-the-story-of-the-mountain-you-climbed-your.

Years ago, I learned the story of my third-great grandmother Catherine Fahy Martin. She was born in Ireland and moved to Scotland where she heard the good news of the gospel of Jesus and was baptized a member of the Church of Jesus Christ of Latter-Day Saints at the age of 21 with her younger sister, Jane, and their brother Samuel. Catherine eventually gathered with other church members in Utah and as she was making the cross-country trek, she took a small tin chest filled with a few beautiful things that helped make the trek more enjoyable for her: face/hand cream, jewelry, colorful silk ribbons, and her high rubber boots. I totally connected with her just in her description of what she took in her cart. I read more stories and connected more deeply. When she grieved, I grieved with her. When she rejoiced, I rejoiced. I told my daughters her stories and they connected with her too. Later, when one of our daughters was a senior in high school, she went through an unusually large number of disappointments. She was really struggling and didn't know how she would make it through these trials. So, I had her read another story of Catherine Fahy.

Catherine and her siblings wanted to gather with the other members of the Church of Jesus Christ of Latter-Day Saints in America to build up Zion. She was working, at the time, in a factory in Lanark, Scotland, but her wages were very low, so as soon as she had earned enough for her younger siblings to make the passage, she sent them to make the journey ahead of herself. Catherine stayed behind to earn enough for her own passage. She moved to Manchester, England where she could earn higher wages and in a few years she had enough to make the trip. The following are the words of Catherine Fahy's granddaughter:

> Finally, the day came when she was to sail for the blessed land of America with a company of Latter-Day Saint emigrants. To her sorrow, unexpected circumstances prevented her from leaving with them. What those unexpected circumstances were, we do not have a record of. The shock and disappointment almost killed her. She grieved terribly and was heartbroken. The Lord comforted her and healed her broken heart. Her

faith had been greatly tried, but the Lord remembered her in her suffering.

One Sunday at church services the power of the Holy Spirit was manifested . . . as a "special blessing for Sister Catherine Faye." In this special blessing, she was told to dry her tears, for the Lord loved and was watching over her; that she was a favored daughter of God whose spirit had been held back to come forth in this last dispensation as she and her seed had a great mission to perform in the gathering and establishment of Israel in these last days. . . . These and many wonderful promises were given and she noted that the blessing to "her seed" was repeated a number of times while as yet she was an unmarried maiden.

Catherine Faye did rejoice in this wonderful blessing. . . . She tried to "dry her tears," but now they were tears of joy, not sorrow.

As our daughter read Catherine's story, she was able to see that she was a descendant of a strong woman who endured and was resilient in those heart-wrenching disappointments. Furthermore, our daughter could see clearly that Catherine's suffering had meaning. Catherine not only endured, but thrived, and so did our daughter.

Catherine finally sailed from Liverpool to New York a full five years after her siblings. In that time, the railroads had been completed into Iowa and she was able to get to Florence Nebraska, shortening her cross-country trek by hundreds of miles. As she was going through her disappointments, she could not have known that 160 years later her story would assist her own family when they were suffering, but I'm so grateful she recorded her story—even when it was painful—because it has the power to heal.

It is through the stories of ancestors that we might find our own story of conquering challenging moments, creating beauty, loving, and being loved. It may be through their stories that we can choose to receive the divine assistance to create meaning and purpose in our lives. I imagine my descendants telling my stories and—seeing my life from beginning to end—easily perceiving the purpose and meaning my life has *now*, and seeing the beauty I created throughout. It reminds me of something C.S. Lewis wrote, "[Mortals] say of some temporal suffering, 'No future bliss can make up for it,' not knowing that Heaven, once attained, will work backwards and turn even that agony into a glory. . . . the Blessed will say, 'We have never lived anywhere except in Heaven.'"[42]

Knowing and telling my current family narrative also has a power with those that are still living the narrative. It can connect me to those that may live far from me or aren't as present in my life. It gives my family a backbone narrative that supports the family and strengthens each member knowing that they are a part of a group that has this rich heritage. In the study called, "Finding Meaning in Difficult Family Experiences: Sense-Making and Interaction Processes During Joint Family Storytelling," the authors found that as families created stories together, their ideas of who they are and who their family is changed.[43]

Tad Callister has taught this truth: "People become more real and relevant in our lives when we know their stories. Stories are a powerful means to convert a lifeless name to a living personality. . . . Our stories have the power to be sermons without preaching. They can inspire us, entertain us, stir emotions, connect our lives to others, bridge the gap of time and distance, and serve as a powerful motivation source for good."[44]

Other studies have suggested that writing about or orally narrating traumatic experiences can have positive effects on individuals' well-being. And the narratives contribute to feelings of understanding, meaning, and control.

According to a study by three Emory psychologists, family stories provide a sense of identity through time, and help children understand who they are in the world. The children who know a lot about

---

42. C.S. Lewis, *The Great Divorce*, (United Kingdom: Geoffrey Bles, 1945).

43. Jody Koenig Kellas and April Trees, "Finding Meaning in Difficult Family Experiences: Sense-Making and Interaction Processes During Joint Family Storytelling," *Journal of Family Communication* 6, no. 1 (January 2006): 49–76, DOI: 10.1207/s15327698jfc0601_4.

44. Marianne Holman Prescott, "RootsTech 2015: Gathering, Healing, and Sealing Families," *Church News*, February 14, 2015, https://www.churchofjesuschrist.org/church/news/rootstech-2015-gathering-healing-and-sealing-families?lang=eng.

their families tend to do better when they face challenges. The more children knew about their family's history, the stronger their sense of control over their lives, the higher their self-esteem, and the more successfully they believed their families functioned.[45]

But the selection of the story is only part of intentional storytelling. Intentional storytelling also includes *how* I tell the story. C. Terry Warner explains in his book *Bonds That Make Us Free,* "It is our presently held story of the past that is our bondage or our freedom."[46] As I understand it, what that means is how I perceive, and tell, the story can allow me to move on, forgive myself and others, and heal—or remain a victim of my past experiences. In other words, if I can look back on my past with gratitude and see it as a great teacher, that is how I "hold" my stories of the past. If, however, I continue to replay the past to find the perpetrator or to find the blame, I can never free myself from the feeling that I *continue* to be a victim of people or experiences in my past. This is not to say that I was never a victim of someone or some situation, but whether I continue to tell the story of my victimhood or tell the story of my forgiveness and redemption, that is a choice that I get to make in the present.

I alluded to this in Chapter 2 (Creativity). After working for a few years as a graphic artist/designer, some of my work was getting noticed and I started to find other designers in my same industry that seemed to be copying my style and "stealing" my ideas. It really bothered me. I felt like something was being taken from me, like I was the victim of their "offense." I would tell this "story" of victim and perpetrator to myself and to Jeff every time it would come up. In an effort to comfort me, Jeff would say something like, "Don't worry, they can copy your designs and maybe your style, but they can't copy the constant flow of ideas that come to you." This helped a bit, but it wasn't until I really internalized the fact that the ideas coming to me were not my own. Their source was the same source of all good things: God. I was just one of many of His children to whom He was sending these beautiful

---

45.   Robyn Fivush, Jennifer Bohanek, and Marshall Duke, "The intergenerational self: Subjective perspective and family history," 2008.

46.   C. Terry Warner, *Bonds That Make Us Free: Healing Our Relationships, Coming to Ourselves* (United States: Shadow Mountain, 2016).

ideas. I began to realize that the same ideas are sent to multitudes of His children, maybe at the same time, and what I did with those that came to me was part of *my* journey of creation. I could not control what anyone else did with them because that was part of *their* creation journey. It was an amazing breakthrough for me and freed me from my victim story. It actually became a story of abundance and love as I started to feel a connection to those of God's children that were receiving, from Him, the beautiful gifts that we shared.

It has served me to ask myself why I'm telling the story. Do I want my audience (this includes myself) to see me as a victim and give me sympathy, or to see me as a hero and give me praise? To see me as better than others so they feel intimidated or less than me? Or is it to allow them to see into my True Self? This is a much more vulnerable type of story. If it's anything but the latter, the story is not expanding my capacities for love and wisdom. It's not allowing my past to strengthen and build me, instead it's allowing my past to keep me captive to limiting beliefs and keep me from feeling my authentic power. Even if I am the only audience of that story, what is the narrative I tell *myself* over and over again? Is it soul expanding or soul shriveling? Is it affirming that authentic power comes from within or feeding the limiting belief that power is outside of me and is either acquired or exercised over me? It's all about *how* I tell my story.

The Lord teaches in stories. Jesus is the Master Storyteller. And all the Lord's stories point us to Him, connect us to Him. They give us a place in the cosmos and allow us to see into the truths that govern life and the universe. The stories Christ tells and the stories that others tell of Him are the stories that I choose to learn those same truths from. The story of miracles, of fasting, of deliverance, of healing, and of creation. It's a pattern that God uses to ensure the continuity of the truths of His plan for us.

When our children were younger, I worked to build God into my stories to illustrate how kind and loving He has been to me. I felt that if they could see that, they would also see Him as kind and loving in their lives.

One of our favorite stories was one of God answering my prayer in an unexpected way. When our girls were little, I took them to a pumpkin patch. It was a beautiful Fall day and the entire patch was strewn with golden hay shining in the sun for that extra Autumn-y atmosphere. It was freezing cold, even though the sun was shining. That's Minnesota for ya! I put one of the girls in a wagon for the pumpkin picking, and as I turned around to grab my other daughter, I felt my diamond wedding ring fly off of my cold fingers. I screamed! Everyone around heard me and we all got on our knees to look for the shiny gold ring in the shiny gold hay. We searched. I prayed. We searched. I prayed some more. We kept searching and I kept praying. I was devastated because we could not find that ring! After doing all we could to find that shiny gold ring in that shiny gold hay—it never turned up.

We drove home and I remember wondering why God hadn't answered my prayers. I had faith. It was a righteous desire to get my wedding ring back, wasn't it? But nothing. As the story unfolded, Jeff told me that he had the ring insured and that we would be able to make a claim and to not worry about it. That relieved me somewhat, but I have to admit, I was still feeling betrayed by God. Why hadn't He answered my prayers?

What I didn't realize is that God had a completely different answer than I thought I wanted. You see, it turned out that when I really thought about getting another diamond wedding ring, it put me in a cold sweat. What if I lost it again? Did I really *need* a diamond? We ended up opting for the insurance claim money and replaced the gold band, sans the diamond (much safer on my hand!). But I still couldn't see God in my story—not until a while later when I had taken Jeff's challenge to start designing my own greeting card line. Remember that?

Turns out, God knew just what we'd need. I was running out of my watercolors and watercolor paper and on our limited grad school budget, I had to get resourceful. In the stacks of library books I scoured through to learn how to get my greeting cards published I found that there was this (relatively) new computer software program called "Photoshop." Apparently this fancy program allowed you to scan your artwork and then manipulate it to create new digital art-work. This was brilliant! I didn't have to buy any more art supplies? There was a way to create my art in new ways and use it over and over? Sign me up!

After reading more I learned that you needed a few things to get started. Not just the Photoshop software, but we needed a computer, monitor, scanner, and a tablet with a stylus to do what I wanted to do. As we looked into it and saw the sticker shock, I thought, "Well, that was a lovely dream." There's no way this was in our budget. But, guess what? God provided a clear means for us to start this dream of mine: the ring money! We were able to buy a used computer, monitor, scanner, and a tablet with a stylus. *And* the Photoshop program—which at the time it was a used version 4.0.

This literally got me started on my journey to creating digital art. There were no online classes, no YouTube, no tutorials in those days. Jeff had to use Photoshop in his graduate work and I remember he showed me the "paint bucket tool" and what it did and away I went. I experimented and worked and taught myself how to use Photoshop. This was the start of Rhonna Designs, and God knew it.

God was always in my story. And after a while I *saw* Him in my story. His answer to my prayers was unexpected, but that answer was a miraculous one. A story of miracles that I shared over and over with our kids as they grew up. Our family knows the power of God's answers in unexpected ways. As I told this story, and so many others, of how God helped me overcome, or deliver, or bring comfort, or perform miracles, I was building God into our story to turn hearts to Him. Our God Story connects us to God.

We always have an audience for our stories. Sometimes ourselves, sometimes our God, sometimes others in our inner circle, sometimes strangers or acquaintances. I love to watch my family and friends as they tell stories. The way they tell a story tells me more about them than the message of the story. It allows me to connect with them through their story.

No matter where I am in my journey, my stories can connect me with my audience, especially when I keep them simple, emotional, true, and real. They become a form of connection, creativity, beauty, and play. They are all intertwined and infuse our "Light Fountain" *with* the Light that shines in our life as we design it.

Principle 6 | SOUL WORK

I give my heart/spirit voice with prayer, scripture,
meditation, and journaling as I create my
story and unlock authentic power.

With appropriate practice in sustaining such higher energies
as love and trust, we increase our capacity to accommodate
increasing heavenly influences. We have already within our
being the energetic seedlings of the attributes of God. They
need only the light of our awareness, a spiritual practice, and
the ever-present enabling power of the Lord.

—M. Catherine Thomas[47]

SOUL WORK IS MY WAY OF SAYING "SPIRITUALITY." IT ENCOMPASSES many of the things that we have already talked about—connecting with my True Self, connecting with the Divine, connecting with the power of my story, and creating beauty in my life. It also encompasses many more things that we get to talk about now, such as finding and creating my true inner voice with prayer, scripture, meditation, and journaling; listening to my heart through experiencing emotions; and living a life full of reverence.

As we begin to talk about Soul Work, it is critical that each of us recognize that we are all on different paths. That one path is not "better" or more "right" than another. My life has a way of teaching

---

47. M. Catherine Thomas, *The God Seed: Probing the Mystery of Spiritual Development.* (United States: Digital Legend, 2014).

exactly in the way that works for me. And though some of my life lessons may be similar to your life lessons, I'm pretty sure the process of arriving at those lessons was very different. Some of us have learned more than others and some have gifts for learning things that others do not. So, I'll speak from a space about what has worked for me and I'll withhold all judgment about others' spiritual progression.

Soul Work, then, is the work or practices that assist me in healing and strengthening my spirit. It is an inner work that manifests through my emotions and outward behavior. This is the work that allows me to realize when I have thoughts that are physically or emotionally harmful or beliefs that limit my spiritual growth. It assists me to see the goals that I intend to achieve in the distant future, while keeping the real work to achieve them in the present, in this very moment. It is the work to progress spiritually.

As we go through some of the practices and experiences that Jeff and I have had, pay attention to your feelings and be open to your heart, to God, and to the Universe. Allow the memories and impressions that you have about improving your own spiritual journey rise to your awareness. Write them down. Make a plan for how you might act on these impressions. And then do it!

The body and the mind are incredible gifts and they really are powerful. Sometimes, if I let them, one or the other will dominate my life. They take over things and become the focus of my activities, thoughts, desires, and intentions. I may forget that they are tools, given to me, merely to assist me in my quest to become like God. I get to remind myself that my mind and my body are not me. They are part of my mortal experience. It was hard for me to recognize that my mind is not who I am, especially since it is constantly telling me things, warning me, analyzing situations, forecasting, and interpreting the world around me. The following is how Jeff has learned to view one function of the mind. I'll let him tell it in his own words:

> I remember first learning about what I'll call the "ego filter"
> a number of years ago. I may have been exposed to it much
> earlier, but it didn't have any meaning for me until a few years
> ago. This "ego filter" is the filter through which I analyze
> everything that comes in through my five senses. The filter is

constructed of my world view, including all my past experiences (which also had to go through the filter), my religious beliefs, my political and philosophical beliefs, the pain or violence I've experienced and all the joys and pleasures as well. Throw in some genetics just to be thorough and the result is the filter through which all of my perceptions are created. The existence of the filter tells me this important truth: what I'm experiencing is not the same as what someone else is experiencing, even if the physical circumstances are identical. It also means that my perceptions are not necessarily aligned with the truth. In fact, they may be so far off the truth that some might wonder if I'm even participating in my own life.

So, what is to be done? How do I get back to the truth? I had to first learn how I can discern the truth. For me, that became a set of practices or processes or a state of being where I am removing or minimizing—even if temporarily—the ego filter that I use to analyze/scrutinize the world. I then work to perceive the world through my heart lens or my soul. By healing those parts of my analytical/evaluative filter that have become damaged by hurt, pain, or violence, I can find a way to open up that analytical filter so that my perception of the world can be open to my heart before it gets clouded. It is a life's work to rid myself of the ego filter and those perceptions that cause my soul to shrivel rather than grow. My mind and body constantly pick up things from this mortal experience that don't serve the True Self, so I want to crack open that filter, so my heart has a chance to lead.

Talking about the heart, though, is a funny thing. In this world of external power structures and hierarchies, it is easy to get labelled a "flaky, starry-eyed dreamer that follows his heart." And it is easy to see why. The heart knows truth and works on a level that is "strange-looking" for those that create their perceptions purely on logic and reasoning based on past experiences with their five physical senses.

But if talking about the heart gave me trouble, getting in touch with my heart felt insurmountable. The reason it was hard for me is because I had suppressed my emotions for so long, I think I forgot how to feel. Without this awareness of my feelings, I was unable to live a life of reverence and compassion. How can I suffer or celebrate with my fellow beings, if I can't feel those emotions for myself?

Many of my practices, now, focus on opening up my heart by allowing myself to feel emotions. It might sound strange to "practice" feeling, but the pathway to the heart is through feeling emotions, and the way to know the truth and perceive truth is by allowing my heart to lead.

Soul Work is the process of working on my soul and heart to expand and connect to my True Self, my God, and others. It's stripping away limiting beliefs that constrict my True Self from rising to my full spiritual stature. I engage in practices that bring my heart, mind, and soul/spirit unified in God's will; letting my spirit guide my mind and body. This unification that I'm talking about is the goal of my Soul Work. It is work guided by my spirit to align with my body and mind so that I can become a Queen and Priestess in the eternities. My Soul Work is an eternal work where I get to learn to listen to my inner voice, which is my spirit/heart connecting with the Holy Spirit and guiding, shaping, and strengthening my body and mind.

It's my spirit and heart, however, that connect directly to God. It's not my body and mind. They can participate, but it's my heart and spirit that make the connection. And it's my heart that connects my True Self to God and others. The ancient prophet Isaiah alluded to this idea as he foretold of the condition of the children of Israel. His prophecy was then repeated by Jesus Christ in the book of Matthew, "This people draweth nigh unto me with their *mouth*, and honoureth me with their lips; but their *heart* is far from me" (Matthew 15:8, emphasis added). There was no connection to God through the heart. Their words and worship were without love.

As we discussed in the "Connection" chapter, these connections to your True Self, to God and others are vital to creativity and inspiration. The inspiration flows when the connections are made. Therefore, I can say that it is through the heart that I receive inspiration. It is through the heart that I am intuitive and receive promptings from

God to serve His children or to make changes in my life to align with Truth and Goodness.

I'm a "feeler." I feel things very deeply in my heart. My motto has always been: "Follow Your Heart." But even as I have followed my heart, I have learned that I must connect my spirit with the Holy Spirit. To me, the Holy Spirit's voice is quiet, positive, loving, and speaks—or shows me in my mind's eye—short, truth-based phrases or actions to do good. When I was in the Missionary Training Center in Provo, Utah as a new missionary, I'll never forget one way the Lord taught me how to hear Him. Our group of missionaries was kneeling in a circle praying for help to learn the Japanese language we had all been called to speak. In my mind, I saw myself standing up after the prayer and telling my companion "Ai shite imasu" (I love you). It was a quiet and fleeting image in my mind's eye. I knew I felt it in my heart to do this, so I did. Later that night in our MTC apartment, she told me she really needed to hear that right at that very moment. Now, I could have easily let the mental chatter of my head overrule my heart and listen to the voice: "That's dumb." "Why would you say that to her? Your Japanese isn't very good." "She might think it's silly," etc. But, in that moment, as I ignored the mental chatter and followed my heart voice instead, I was hearing Him. Through the years, His voice has gotten more clear, more steady, and I'm hearing Him in even more ways. Becoming fluent in Japanese was not my gift, but I'm becoming more fluent in the language of His Voice and that means everything.

So, what is this mental chatter that seems to argue with the messages I receive in my heart? I'm calling it "the voice in my head." It is constantly talking about what I'm doing; why I'm doing it; why I shouldn't be doing it; why I should do it differently. It tells me why I should feel dumb, embarrassed, or regret things I've said. It reminds me what I should have done or said; tells me why I'm not good enough; reminds me of my weaknesses or other people's weaknesses. Sometimes it's just chattering away. Sometimes it's battering! I recognize it is the same voice and it is almost constant. Michael Singer, in *The Untethered Soul*[48], explains the voice and asks the reader

---

48. Michael A. Singer, *The Untethered Soul: The Journey Beyond Yourself* (Oakland, CA: New Harbinger Publications, 2007).

who is talking. And who is *it* talking to? He points out very clearly that the voice is not *me*. The voice is talking *to* me. But the voice is not me. I am the one hearing the voice. So, what is the voice? The voice is coming from my head and it's talking or trying to talk to my True Self. But there's another "voice." It's not constant. It doesn't chatter or batter. It doesn't even necessarily have words, and it originates in my heart. It only tells the Truth, and it has taken me years to recognize it and listen.

The heart speaks to me through feelings. It gives me the feeling to do something good like reach out to a friend, go talk to the new neighbor, call my mom. But then the other voice starts its chatter. It tells me why I shouldn't do it and brings out all the doubts. "It's just a feeling," it says. "I just made it up myself," it says. Like Jeff says he likes to think of the voice in his head as a little guy who's telling him stuff constantly—some of it is useful, most of it is garbage, and some of it is downright dark. Then there's the heart. He says he thinks of it as a big lovable guy giving him the impression/feeling that he should do something that serves him, serves others, or both. He says his heart is not loud and, as of now, it has no clear voice spoken in English. Its messages feel more like something leaning on him, pushing gently, nudging him to do something good or to grow in some fashion. Sometimes the voice in my head would agree with the impressions from my heart, but most of the time the voice is analyzing the impressions and creating doubts and fear based on past experiences and limiting beliefs. When I started feeling and knowing the difference between the two voices, the scriptures describing the still small voice take on greater meaning:

> . . . They heard a voice as if it came out of heaven; and they cast their eyes round about, for they understood not the voice which they heard; and it was not a harsh voice, neither was it a loud voice; nevertheless, and notwithstanding it being a small voice it did pierce them that did hear to the center, insomuch that there was no part of their frame that it did not cause to quake; yea, it did pierce them to the very soul, and did cause their hearts to burn. And it came to pass that again they heard the voice, and they understood it not. And again the third

time they did hear the voice, and did open their ears to hear it; and their eyes were towards the sound thereof; and they did look steadfastly towards heaven, from whence the sound came. And behold, the third time they did understand the voice which they heard; and it said unto them: Behold my Beloved Son, in whom I am well pleased, in whom I have glorified my name—hear ye him.[49]

It sounds a bold thing to say but it is true: the head is *believing*, while the heart is *knowing*. When bearing testimony, *I can* say "I know" because it's coming from my heart. Jeff's experience as a scientist created a bit of a hurdle for him to understand the difference between the two voices:

My academic training taught me to experience life through the mind and the physical senses and believe that if you can't taste, test, touch, see or hear it that it can't be known. And for many years I struggled hearing people say in their testimonies "I know." I was the guy thinking, "You can't know unless you've done the experiment and can prove it." But I'm so grateful that time and experience have shown otherwise. It still serves me in many circumstances to think and believe with my head, but the aim of my Soul Work is to master my thoughts and start feeling more. I love this quote from M. Catherine Thomas in her article titled *The Illusion of Fear*:

The Lord says, "Be still and know that I am God." (Psalm 46:10). It is in the stillness of our own soul that we know Him, that we find the Lord if we are looking for him. Within our soul is the sacred sanctuary of our own True Self, and connected with that, the conscious presence of the Lord Himself. Closer than our breath, more intimate than anything within or without, is this loving, patient, Presence—waiting for our conscious awareness. Perhaps for the very reason that it is so close, we are not often aware of it. What's beautiful about this is that communing with the Lord

---

49. 3 Nephi 11:3–7.

isn't so much a matter of trying to get the attention of a God "out there," as it is to remove the things in here that are in the way of our perceiving His presence— that "veil of unbelief."[50]

Since Pres. Nelson gave me the commandment to "Hear Him," referring to my Savior, Jesus Christ, I have learned that I hear Him through my *heart voice*. That He speaks to my heart. For me, if I want to hear Him, I listen to my heart. It often takes time to quiet the other voice, to get in tune with feelings or "senses" (other than the five physical senses) and then start to write what I feel. Pausing at times to quiet myself again. It is a beautiful and sacred process for me and I'm grateful that I was open to it. Now, when bearing my witness of the Savior I *can* say "I know" because it's coming from my heart.

Soul Work strengthens my ability to perceive the world through my heart. And it opens up the filter that my mind has constructed based on past experiences and limiting beliefs. It assists me to recognize and stay in authentic power which is the power to love and feel loved, to accept and feel accepted, to know intuitively things that are true, to create beauty, and to change my perception of the world.

---

50. M. Catherine Thomas, "The Illusion of Fear," *Meridian Magazine*, March 10, 2016, https://ldsmag.com/the-illusion-of-fear/.

How do we *do* Soul Work?

---

*"When human beings become still, they go beyond thought.
There is an added dimension of knowing, of awareness,
in the stillness that is beyond thought."*

—Eckhart Tolle[51]

Meditation/Stillness/Prayer

There are many ways to practice connecting to your True Self and the Divine. Both Jeff and I use meditation as part of Soul Work.

Jeff explains Soul Work meditation like this:

> I like to sit cross-legged with my back straight so that I can breathe more easily. I tried doing it laying down, which is more comfortable, but once I was able to quiet my mind, I would fall right to sleep. So, if I'm *not* looking for a nap, I sit up straight. Then I work on quieting my mind, quieting the voice and all the thoughts in my head. I sometimes use focal points to do this. I'll focus on my breath or I'll focus on the top of my head or my spine. And then I just sit and keep quiet for as long as it serves me. Then I'll run through some affirmations, taking time between to refocus and re-quiet my mind. After the affirmations, and when I'm ready, I'll go into prayer and ask what we'll be working on that day and then listen for promptings. And lest you think I'm some kind of meditation master, most days I struggle to stay quiet. Some days I feel rushed. Some days I don't feel like doing it at all, so I like to mix in some yoga or other exercises so that it doesn't become too routine.
>
> I'm surprised at the difference it makes in my day to take this time in the morning. If I'm rushing out to something, I may do it at noon (I'm definitely dozing off for that session). When I started practicing meditation, I honestly could not

---

51. Eckhart Tolle, *Stillness Speaks* (Vancouver: Namaste Publishing, 2003), 85.

figure out why having a completely empty mind for several minutes a day was a good thing, but there I was feeling better, thinking more clearly and becoming more aware and more present. Things in my life really started to change. I remember starting to feel an awareness of my spirituality. I started to perceive when certain things weren't working for me and I felt like I knew what to do to change them to start working. I love this quote from C.S. Lewis:

> . . . [T]he real problem of the Christian life comes where people do not usually look for it. It comes the very moment you wake up each morning. All your wishes and hopes for the day rush at you like wild animals. And the first job each morning consists simply in shoving them all back; in listening to that other voice, taking that other point of view, letting that other larger, stronger, quieter life come flowing in. And so on, all day. Standing back from all your natural fussings and frettings; coming in out of the wind. We can only do it for moments at first. But from those moments the new sort of life will be spreading through our system: because now we are letting Him work at the right part of us.[52]

When I'm in a space of love, connection, peace, and humility I can let my heart lead. In order to get into that space, I wake up and pray immediately. Then, I meditate and move my body. This allows my body, heart, and spirit to come together. I speak one sentence over and over in my mind. Some days I will repeat, "I love and accept you, Rhonna." Other days I will repeat, "I'm a radiant covenant-keeping daughter of God." Or it may be a phrase from my personal mission statement, "I access Christ's power and partner with Him to activate my Divine Gifts." In these quiet, still moments I imagine my spirit connecting with the Holy Spirit and ask for Christ's atoning power to enable me to live out my full purpose on the earth. This allows me to hear my heart voice and follow my heart, and intuition throughout the day.

---

52. C.S. Lewis, *Mere Christianity* (New York: HarperCollins, 2001), 198.

Affirmations

---

*"I AM are two of the most powerful words, for
what you put after them shapes your reality."*

—Anonymous

*"Instead of worrying about what you cannot control,
shift your energy to what you can create."*

—Roy T. Bennett[53]

Affirmations are an incredibly powerful tool I use as part of my Soul Work. Actually, every person with a normally functioning brain is using "affirmations" to some extent. Remember the "little voice in my head" that Jeff described. That little voice, which is an almost universal part of being human, is constantly reciting "affirmations." The question is, what kind of affirmations is it reciting to me?

I remember moments in my life when I was told I didn't have the ability to do something—it doesn't matter who said it or what it was. This untruth wedged in my conscious and my subconscious. I held onto it and started to believe it. This is called a limiting belief. I was in the habit of reinforcing this limiting belief by saying it over and over all day long. I would repeat in my mind all the things I wasn't good at, the things I should do better, how I wasn't capable, how I couldn't be happy if life didn't meet my expectations, how life is so hard, or how I'm so sick. I didn't realize these were negative affirmations that were constant in my mind. One major source of these negative affirmations was my limiting beliefs about my body. I constantly fought my body. I didn't like the way it looked or the way I felt. I'd take drastic measures to be happy in my body. The energy I used and the hours of expending that energy through the years is mind boggling. By repeating this mental batter, my negative affirmations were realized and my body, spirit, and mind suffered for it.

Finally, I woke up and realized I could gain the power over this negative thinking and I had the ability to make significant positive

---

53. Roy T. Bennett, *The Light in the Heart* (Self-published, 2020), 33.

changes in my mind, body and spirit. How? By serious reflection in myself. By overriding those deeply rooted fears and limiting beliefs and connecting with my True Self and God like never before. My *body* started responding to these positive affirmations and I stepped into my power. My *spirit* was set free when I started leaning into my daily positive affirmations and as I trained my *mind* with these powerful words. I was re-building myself to rise to my full spiritual stature. Shifting this inner dialogue was a game changer. I'm grateful I chose to let God change my thinking and He changed my life by reminding me who I truly am.

Personal Mission Statement

A personal mission statement is my statement of purpose—the purpose for my life. It is something that can be developed during those quiet, peaceful moments that one feels very close to God. And it will likely change over time. Jeff explains his this way:

> I constructed a personal mission statement with the assistance of some very good life coaches. The words that I used came as an impression to my heart and they are very true to my soul. Every time I say them, which is at least daily, my heart reminds me of their truthfulness, and I feel the power of the words giving me permission to actualize them in my life. So, I usually repeat them as part of meditation and focus on the meaning of each word and visualize what it looks like to be that.

My personal mission statement allows me to recenter my focus on what I consider to be most important and assists me to rein in activities or thoughts that are taking me too far from the stated purpose.

When I was getting my degree in art, one of my professors introduced me to something like a personal mission statement. It wasn't called that, but it was a statement of who I am—my values, goals and aspirations—and what I wanted to become and accomplish as an artist. That was the seed of a personal mission statement, and through the years I have incorporated this tool into my personal and business life. It has taken many different forms and has been revised numerous times, but I've always had a guiding statement for my life. It became even more significant to me when President Russell M. Nelson, in a talk given in the October 2018 General Conference, said, "I urge you to study the current Relief Society purpose statement. It is inspiring. *It may guide you in developing your own purpose statement for your own life.*"[54] I then made the effort to fast and to pray, and really look at my personal mission statement from a spiritual perspective.

Power Phrases/Power Stances

Power phrases and power stances draw upon the idea that the mind and the body are powerful tools that I can use to create change in the moment. To illustrate the power of the mind as a tool to immediately change your emotional state or your energy, think about a time when someone told you something incredibly good or incredibly bad. Here are some examples:

"Hi, Mom, Dad? I just got in an accident."
"You're pregnant!" or "I'm pregnant!"
"You got the job!"
"The repair will be $4000."
"You won!"
"I didn't make the team."
"I got fired today."
"They loved the presentation, and we got the account!"
"Can you speak in church on Sunday?"

Notice the immediate shift these phrases potentially have on the energy or emotional state of the one receiving the information. These are *external* "power phrases" that life occasionally presents to us. They have a very real effect in the moment that we hear them, even if we find out later that they weren't true. It's incredible that a few simple words can completely change the mindset or emotional state of a person but notice also that some of those phrases could "trigger" the opposite response in two different people. There is still a choice to be

---

54. Russell M. Nelson, "Sisters' Participation in the Gathering of Israel," *Ensign*, November 2018.

made and action to be taken by the receiver. The phrase is just the tool to initiate that choice or action.

Now think of using that same power whenever you feel that a shift in energy or emotion would serve you in the moment. I harness this power all the time by using power phrases that I have made up. They are similar to affirmations, but they are more of a quick booster shot of energy. When I am feeling low on energy, openness, love, or joy, I can use these power phrases to shift my vibration back in alignment with my intentions and mission statement and bring my awareness back to the present moment. The effect is almost immediate. Power phrases need little explanation or evidence. You say them, you feel the energy, and it works.

The power stance is similar to the power phrase, but it includes the body in shifting my energy. Which one I use depends on the situation. In the earlier years of my life, I was absolutely terrified of speaking in front of people, to the point of making myself sick if I knew a speaking assignment was approaching. While I was serving a mission in Japan, I learned through the Holy Spirit that one of my gifts was speaking and testifying of truth. I spent a good deal of time on my knees asking God how I could make this seeming weakness into a strength. One of the things He taught me was power stances. Before I go to speak in front of an audience (big or small), I find a mirror or a place where I can do a few power poses. If I am speaking with another person, I'll invite them to join me. I found that it assists both of us to speak with greater power and it brings connection and unity to the moment.

Obviously, there are times that the power stance would not seem appropriate. I've been on a stage or a stand waiting to speak and felt the need for a little boost, so I'll say power phrases in my mind and I'll say a prayer and ask to speak with God's power and authority. That's a serious power phrase!

Jeff explains one of his power phrases this way:

I can really get down on myself sometimes, especially when I know that I've made a critical error either socially, financially, or whatever. I will go through the process of forgiving myself and, if necessary, seeking reconciliation with someone I've offended, but even after that, I'll still feel low. I'm feeling the resistance of life or the twinge of reminder that I've still got a lot to learn. So, to get my energy back up, I'll use my power phrases. As an example, I might exclaim, *"This is exciting! This is easy! This is fun!"* three times out loud, followed by saying *"Yes!"* three times with a fist pump. I use power phrases to give me that "push" to shift my own energy. The phrases and fist pumps don't shift my energy for me. I still have to decide to shift it myself, but the power phrases and power poses assist me in that shift.

The key to unlocking the power of these tools is sincerity and speaking them (or acting them) from the heart. I have to believe the words and feel the energy. I don't say it and then wait for the energy to shift—I say it and shift my energy. Like Jeff said, the power phrase or power stance is the "push" that assists me to shift my energy.

One Word

This is my yearly intention of what I want to grow into. I use it daily in my affirmations, intentions, my prayer, and meditation. It becomes my power word that I incorporate into every facet of my life (e.g. this year is "Abundance"). When I found my word (and it found me), I recognized it immediately. It built on past years' words and as I look back, I see how God has led me each year as I intentionally focus on one word to step into my True Self.

Intention

Another practice is to clearly set an intention for that day and very purposefully not focus on the mechanics of how I'm going to accomplish the intention. Then allow my heart to push myself forward—to proceed with faith and knowledge. Faith that my heart knows what to do. Faith that I'm receiving messages from the Spirit, that will let the mechanics fall in place.

Jeff says that when he gets a prompting and that becomes his intention, the "other" voice comes up and starts to tell him all the reasons he should *not* do what he's about to do. When he hears that voice, he'll thank the voice and tell it, "It's probably right, but we are going to do this anyway." In that way there is no argument with the voice because the voice will always come up with an argument to not do what the heart tells me to do.

What does prayer, scripture study, or journaling look like in this process?

For me, I connect and create through prayer with my God. I learn His story and teachings through His scriptures and as I receive the Word, it allows me to connect with my God and my faith story. My meditation is a creation in my heart, mind, and soul that assists me to transcend and overcome my limiting beliefs and access the power of Jesus Christ's Atonement. My journaling is a way to manifest and create intention, record my story, thoughts, and feelings, and to assist me to see the beauty and power of my story and design my life in beautiful and meaningful ways.

There are so many practices that can assist the person that is working toward greater spirituality and greater connection to Self, God, and others. These are a few that we have found to be of great value and effectiveness to us. We have added these practices to our traditional religious practices, which have already and continue to benefit our spiritual journey. For you, the practices here may be old, or they may be new. Our goal is to share our experience in the hope that you might find something of value to add to your practice of Soul Work.

I want to end this chapter with something Jeff shared with me:

When Rhonna and I first discussed the ideas in this chapter, I had no doubts that she was correct in her assertions that Soul Work, as she describes it here, enhanced creativity and inspiration, after all she had the credibility when it came to those things, and I had begun to experience greater inspiration and creativity as I settled into my own practice of Soul Work. So I knew it was true, but the scientist in me wanted to know how exactly it happens and if it was possible to explain it. Part of the explanation, for me, was found in what I've called the ego filter. If I'm filtering my present experiences through only past experiences, and my belief system, then I have a *limited* perspective. It's likely a perspective based on fear and doubt because my head is attempting to protect me from present experiences using my perception of past experiences, which also could be incomplete and skewed by even further past experiences. By healing or opening up that filter, my heart begins to take a larger, and eventually the dominant, part of creating my perspectives. It is opening myself up to unlimited possibilities and unlimited perspectives. This has led, for me, to a greater openness to new experiences and connecting with new people. It has shifted my perspective of life from whatever it was, to a great adventure full of possibilities, creativity, inspiration, and beauty.

I have had the sacred privilege of watching this amazing change in Jeff's life. We both are learning to live a life full of reverence. Reverence is not a behavior. It's a state of mind or feeling that is reflected in behavior. It's an attitude, an awareness. But, more than that, it's an *awareness* of the divinity of life. Gary Zukav explained in *The Seat of the Soul,* "We see that when the activities of life are infused with reverence, they come alive with meaning and purpose. We see that when reverence is lacking from life's activities, the result is cruelty, violence, and loneliness."[55]

For me, to live a life of reverence is to see it as sacred and holy. To see life in the way I see the Savior—with love and gratitude. This learning experience called life is made possible through Jesus Christ. So, I choose to see my life infused with divinity so that my "Light Fountain" is showering me with light—God's light. It is all around me and passing through me. God has put His mark on everything in my life, every experience, and every moment. My very soul is imbued with divinity. That is how reverence *feels* to me—confessing the divinity in all things. Then allowing God's will to direct my path.

---

55. Gary Zukav, *The Seat of the Soul* (United States: Simon & Schuster, 2007), 6.

Principle 7 | ABUNDANCE

*I create "plenty" of time, energy, value,
effort, ideas, inspiration.*

---

*"It would seem that Our Lord finds our desires not
too strong, but too weak. We are half-hearted creatures,
fooling about with drink and sex and ambition when
infinite joy is offered us, like an ignorant child who wants
to go on making mud pies in a slum because he
cannot imagine what is meant by the offer of a
holiday at the sea. We are far too easily pleased."*

—C.S. Lewis[56]

I REMEMBER HEARING THE PHRASE "THE LAW OF ABUNDANCE" AND honestly, not knowing what it meant. I had heard a similar phrase—"Abundance Mentality"—when I was serving the people of Okinawa, Japan. Someone talked about having an "Abundance Mentality" while serving as a missionary teaching gospel of Jesus, but I still didn't quite "get it." In college I heard about Stephen R. Covey's book: *7 Habits for Highly Effective People*[57] and was introduced to an "Abundance Mentality" vs. a "Scarcity Mentality."

In his book, Covey used the term "Abundance Mentality" or "Abundance Mentality" to describe the mental state of believing that there are plenty of resources and that success for one individual does

---

56. C.S. Lewis, *The Weight of Glory* (United States: HarperOne, 2009), 26.
57. Stephen R. Covey, *The Seven Habits of Highly Effective People* (United States: Simon and Schuster, 1989).

not take away from the possibility of success for others. In other words, successes are plentiful and can be shared with many or even all. Covey also used the term "Scarcity Mentality" to describe the belief that successes and resources are limited and the more one person has of either of those things, the less another is able to have or experience. The Scarcity Mentality doesn't allow the possibility that everyone can experience success or that everyone can win.

For many people, the Law of Abundance is exclusively associated with resources. But I have learned that it has to do with health, time, love, energy, creativity, and inspiration. The Law of Abundance implies that there is more than enough of all of those things for all of God's children. Some might ask if the Law of Abundance is *believing* you have more than enough or *really* having more than enough. I'll answer that question as soon as someone satisfactorily explains the difference. There are those who, from my perspective, may not appear to have enough and yet feel that they are overflowing with blessings and resources. To the point that they are sharing and giving with what little they *seem* to have. And then there are those that, again from my perspective, appear to have more than they could enjoy in a thousand lifetimes, and yet feel that they need more. To the point that they might even take from others.

As a college student in the Art Education program, this idea of abundance was something really significant to me. When I stood up in front of my colleagues to "defend" my art pieces, it really served me to focus on the concept of believing there is enough success for everyone in that room. But I found myself, and my colleagues, really having to fight the tendency to give in to destructive—and certainly unnecessary—competition. We were all learning together as we fought back the feelings of losing when others would critique our beloved art pieces.

It was an amazing learning experience for me, but as I worked to apply this Abundance Mentality more broadly in my life, I found that it wasn't always very obvious or easy. As the years have gone by, and I've learned more and more about Abundance, I have found that I can explain it best in one word: feeling. It's an expansive feeling. The same kind of expansive feeling when I am feeling intense gratitude or trust. It *affects* my heart and mind and it's pretty obvious to me now when I am in an abundance mindset or a scarcity mindset because it either feels like my heart and mind are expanding or it feels like they are contracting.

Clearly perspective is a large part of an Abundance Mentality, ot the Law of Abundance. I believe this quote from Eckhart Tolley is key to understanding abundance: "Acknowledging the good that you already have in your life is the foundation for all abundance."[58] The message is not only one of perspective, but also gratitude. How can I acknowledge the good in my life without creating the feeling of gratitude?

We have found that another part of The Law of Abundance is that if we allow good things to flow from us, good things will flow to us. Stopping that flow, either to or from, stops the abundance. My experience is that it takes courage to implement this concept—courage and trust. Courage to let go of the good things, that maybe I have worked really hard to obtain, and trust that good things really will flow back into my life.

Abundance has always been a tough thing to talk about because there is a stigma in my mind surrounding this topic. It feels a bit like I'm boasting about my wealth or prosperity if I say, "We have enough money." Or if I say that I have enough time, am I not keeping myself busy? Do I need more work to do? Am I idle? And if I say that I have plenty of energy or health, am I going to make unhealthy people feel bad? It's as if stating my abundance isn't humility. Obviously, my intentions behind the statements determine whether it was said in humility or out of pride, but as I started to learn more about the Law of Abundance, I realized the possibility that I was really expressing my own limiting beliefs.

As we brought up our children, Jeff had a saying he borrowed from Richard Bach, he liked to use with our kids. "Argue for your limitations and sure enough they're yours."[59] He would tell them, "If you say you can't, you're right." I remember how it would make our

---

58.   Eckhart Tolle, *A New Earth: Awakening to Your Life's Purpose* (United Kingdom: Penguin Publishing Group, 2006), 190.
59.   Richard Bach, *Illusions: The Adventures of a Reluctant Messiah* (United Kingdom: Penguin Publishing Group, 2012).

kids roll their eyes at the time, but each one of them has repeated it at some point as a source of inspiration. It made me stop and think too. I recognized I was hearing some limiting arguments in my own mental chatter that would actually come out in my conversations: *I'm too busy. I can't afford that. I'm too sick to do that.* Yup, I said those phrases a lot. Too much. Rather than showing humility, expressing scarcity was my way of arguing for my limitations. And the limitations, unfortunately, had become mine.

If I say I don't have enough time to do something, I'm right. If I say I don't have enough money to buy something, I'm right. If I say I don't have enough energy, I'm right. I recognized this wasn't serving me. I wanted to shift my mindset. But how? I started to take those limiting statements and reshape them into words of abundance. I started using them in my daily affirmations and intentions and soon, I was right.

Some of you reading this might say, "but I really *don't* have enough money to buy this thing I really want . . . *and I am right!*" Well, all I can suggest is think about the focus of this statement and feel the power that you are giving to it. Also, think about the hold that it may have on your life and what your life might look like if that were not one of your strongly held beliefs. We all have a favorite thing or two that we really feel is scarce in our lives. Mine was health and time. I have always told myself I'm too tired or sick and I wore "not enough time" like a badge of honor.

The source of Jeff's feeling of scarcity has always been money. He really has a gift for managing and saving money, but like many of our gifts, when we are in fear, the gift becomes a weakness. He too uses affirmation statements, but he had an analogy come to him and he uses it as a tool during the day to keep him feeling the abundance of life. The simple analogy is this:

> An employee is asked by The Company to travel far from his home to start up and finish a project. The employee will be starting with nothing at the site, but The Company is providing a budget and timeframe to complete the project. The Company also provides compensation for his travel and living expenses while he's there. If the project goes over the

time or over the budget, The Company assures him that they will extend the time and the budget. Obviously being a good steward of the finances is important, but the employee realizes that his extreme frugality in this scenario may not serve the project, and in turn, The Company. For example, buying the cheapest equipment may result in lost time due to equipment failures and increased costs due to repairs, etc.

When Jeff told me this analogy, he went on for quite some time elaborating on the details. He went through multiple examples of how a scarcity mindset with regards to money would hurt the project; how the employee would want to focus on quality equipment, supplies, workers, etc. to maximize the quality of the results; and that money saved on the budget would not excuse an unfinished or failed project. Then he stopped and asked me, "Aren't I on that jobsite right now? Isn't my life the assignment to go far from 'home' and accomplish the project that God has for me? Do I not trust that God will provide what is required for me to finish the project in both time and resources? And don't all of these resources belong to God?" I could tell these thoughts had an impact on him and he has changed his mindset. He is still really good with money, but he is free of the burden of concern that stems from the fear of scarcity. Every now and then, when he slips back into "scarcity" and is struggling to spend money on something, I can literally see him surrender his anxiety and relax into the moment. Then he'll look at me with a smile and say, "It's for The Company."

Now we are both finding the "Law of Abundance" permeating every aspect of our lives. There are an abundance of ideas, possibilities, connections, and friends. There's an abundance of beauty, learning, and experience. It infuses even our consciousness—our very identity.

Why is it important?

In terms of creativity, the Law of Abundance allows those creative muscles to expand. It frees me from the limiting belief that something is "mine" and no one else can have it or copy it. It gives me the knowledge that if there's an abundance for me, then there is an abundance for everyone. So, the same ideas that are coming to me are coming to thousands or millions or more. I love this quote from Jen Hatmaker: "This life is not a race or a contest, there is enough abundance to go around, your seat at the table is secure, and you have incredible gifts to offer. You are not in competition with your peers."[60] I am not in competition and I have no need to feel threatened because we are all connected by the Light of Christ. Elder Boyd K Packer said,

> The Spirit of Christ can enlighten the inventor, the scientist, the painter, the sculptor, the composer, the performer, the architect, the author to produce great, even inspired things for the blessing and good of all mankind.
>
> This Spirit can prompt the farmer in his field and the fisherman on his boat. It can inspire the teacher in the classroom, the missionary in presenting his discussion. It can inspire the student who listens. And of enormous importance, it can inspire husband and wife, and father and mother.[61]

As an artist/designer, one of the really fun things for me was seeing my work reproduced on a product, but as a young, "still-learning" designer I remember getting really upset when I would see other designers "copying" my designs or my style and then seeing those designs having success. I felt cheated. I felt robbed and I didn't like the way it felt. Then there was a time that I was accused of copying someone else's work. I was absolutely offended. Never in my life would I even think of taking someone's design. How could they possibly accuse me of that?

Being on the receiving side of the accusation gave me a different perspective. The reality is that styles trend, fads are real, and many designers will converge on a similar style either because it's trending or they just happen to have similar styles. I'm sure there are many cases where a designer really does copy or steal from another designer, but now I know that similar ideas come to many people at once and I have

---

60. Jen Hatmaker, *Of Mess and Moxie: Wrangling Delight Out of This Wild and Glorious Life* (United States: Thomas Nelson, 2017), xvi.
61. Boyd K. Packer, "The Light of Christ" [address at a seminar for new mission presidents, Missionary Training Center, Provo, UT, June 22, 2004].

learned to say, there is enough for everyone: enough ideas, enough creativity, and enough room for everyone to enjoy success.

I recall a time, years ago, Jeff and I had this pivotal discussion. He was working at his first job after graduate school and my little business of designing greeting cards and gift wrap/bags had grown to include designing scrapbooking supplies. I don't remember the exact subject of the discussion, but it usually revolved around money. Were they paying enough? How much should I ask for? Are they ripping us off? Are we ripping them off? What does the contract say? Is that fair? And etc. I remember that this discussion was something to do with making a decision to do a project for a certain amount or whether or not to pursue something for the pay level/value that they were promising. And in a moment of clarity, Jeff said something that was so uncharacteristic for him, that to this day, I'm surprised he said it. He told me that we were blessed to have a salaried job to pay the bills and provide a good life for our young family, and he encouraged me to stop thinking about the money and just focus on being the best at what I do. And that I should accept any project that would allow me to be creative, enjoy the process, and work at being my best. In that moment I could feel his commitment and sincerity and I felt my own stress over chasing money dissipate. It hadn't been that long since we were in graduate school with little to no money, so this notion of not worrying about it was new to us and I probably gave him a strange look.

I know it was one of those pivotal moments. I could feel myself let go, like when you realize you have been tightening your shoulder muscles throughout an entire action movie and now the movie's over and you feel yourself relax. Jeff's suggestion to *not* focus on money eliminated the "money is scarce" mindset as my motivation for designing. It changed everything and it became the basis for our decisions surrounding my design business.

The irony in including that experience in a chapter on abundance is that Jeff's suggestion was made without explicitly thinking about the Law of Abundance. What we have learned since that moment, so many years ago, is that I didn't need to wait until Jeff had his "steady" job to drop my scarcity mindset surrounding money and to stop focusing on money as the motivation for my business decisions. Because as I shifted my focus to being creative, enjoying the process and being my best, my business began to flourish to a degree that neither of us expected. The scarcity mindset that we had been operating under ensured that money would stay "scarce." Looking back, I see the whole experience was a huge teaching moment for both of us. God, in His mercy, was allowing us to take some tiny steps toward understanding His incredible abundance.

How do we live in abundance?

Practice.

The life change from scarcity to abundance is like learning a foreign language; it may take a long time and a lot of practice to master the language, but the decision to start learning that language can happen in a moment. Shifting to the path of abundance is something I can choose to do now. The first step of creation is in my thoughts, then in my words. (Remember, "watch yourselves, and your thoughts, and your words, and your deeds.") Then I act on the thoughts and words I have, and I start creating abundance in my life. Starting with the easy things, really taking baby steps, is important to me.

So, the first step is making the decision to change. Next is practicing gratitude. Create a gratitude journal; put up a blank poster board on the wall and every time you walk in the room write something down for which you are thankful; create daily lists of things you are thankful for about your life, about your job, about your family, about your spouse. Mention the things you are grateful for to friends, family, or on social media.

The next step in the change is working on trust. How can you increase in trust? For both Jeff and me, it took the practice of meditation and daily affirmations to increase our trust. Where is this trust placed? It is placed in God. It is placed in the Universe and it is placed in the Law of Abundance.

The process of increasing trust happens as you eliminate the scarcity mindset. Start by looking at the places where you are really feeling scarcity and start creating your words that support your shift to abundance. The daily affirmations are very powerful in steering your heart and mind to a place of abundance. Work to eliminate the words to which you are conditioned that strengthen the scarcity mindset. Start your scarcity mindset abstinence program as soon as you see the areas in your life where you feel scarcity, and be open to what those might be: health, time, money, attention, ideas, creativity, or love.

Begin with something easy. Ask, "Where can I start to create abundance today?" Learn to use your words to manifest your intentions, desires, and shape your abundant life with faith in Christ. One way to do this is to speak and act as though the thing you are manifesting has already occurred or is already present in your life. In other words, instead of "One day I'll learn to play the guitar," you say, "I play the guitar." Instead of "One day I'll write a book," it's, "I am a writer." Obviously, the only way you can say those things in honesty is if you are currently writing or playing the guitar, regardless of how often or the quality of the results. Practice believing it is so. Your words and thoughts can assist you, so think it, speak it, and do it.

You will start noticing how abundance feels compared with scarcity, and you will also have moments when you slip back into old habits of scarcity. That is okay. That is the resistance that life is offering to you so that you can become stronger. It may serve you to have things to remind you of your changing mindset. Confiding in someone close to you and asking them to keep you accountable can be a great tool in staying on course. It also gives you someone to talk to and share some encouraging words with when you are feeling the resistance or discouragement. Just make sure it's someone that won't acquiesce and tell you that you're justified in reverting to your old ways.

The idea, for me, was to practice letting go—not just of resources, but of limiting beliefs and fears. In Kimberly Giles's book, *Choosing Clarity*,[62] she points out that the two core fears are the fear that you might not be good enough and the fear of loss, or the fear that your life isn't going to be good enough. Notice that both fears have a statement of limitation—"not good enough." Letting go of fears, regardless of which core fear they are based on, allows me to rid myself of those limitations.

---

62. Kimberly Giles, *Choosing Clarity: The Path to Fearlessness* (United States: Thomas Noble Books, 2014.)

I found it very useful in constructing my affirmations to take the very limiting beliefs that I had told myself and inverting them to create the affirmation. For example, "I don't have the time" became "I am grateful for all the time I have to do exactly what God needs me to do." The phrase, "I don't have enough money" became "I am grateful for all the money I have to serve, love, and build God's kingdom," and from "I don't have the energy," I created "I am grateful for all the energy Christ has infused into my body, heart, and spirit. I can do anything He leads me to do." Using these daily affirmation statements has assisted me to shift my thinking, and it has changed everything for me.

Another tool that I have used to assist me in maintaining an abundance mindset is a vision board. A vision board is something you create by collecting and assembling any number of images, artwork, quotes, etc. onto one poster or wall or canvas. It can be used to display the things that bring you joy or matter most to you. It can be used to give you inspiration, keep you grounded, remind you of your goals, or many other positive things. There is actually a very popular social media platform that many people use to create vision boards. I love to use my mobile device apps, Rhonna Designs and Rhonna Collage to create vision boards. But a vision board doesn't need to be just images or even limited to the visual sense. Vision boards can include quotes or inspiring words, or they can be a playlist of music.

I like to use what I call a *living* vision board. I call it "living" because it is constantly growing and evolving. The idea behind a vision board is to continually keep my vision clear and focused. So just as I must continually change the prescription for my eyeglasses as my vision changes, I also continually update, change, and create completely new vision boards as my perspectives, goals, or desires change.

My living vision board for an abundance mindset would include images or quotes that evoke images of the changes that I'm making. It would include colors and patterns that get me motivated and excited to keep growing and keep improving. It would include my One Word for this year, which happens to be "Abundance."

Jeff's path to abundance started by recognizing that there were material things that he had collected over the years, for their value, but that were creating a feeling of attachment, so he simply began to give them away. He then began meditating as a way to practice love and gratitude, release his fears, and increase his trust in God. He has adopted some of my practices, and I his, but we both watch closely the words we choose, knowing the powerful influence they have on the mind, and we both practice optimism. On being optimistic, Gordon B Hinckley wrote:

> In my 90-plus years, I have learned a secret. I have learned that when good men and good women face challenges with optimism, things will always work out! Truly, things always work out. Despite how difficult circumstances may look at the moment, those who have faith and move forward with a happy spirit will find that things always work out."[63]

In Jeff's last semester teaching at the university, he decided to experiment with his class. He walked in the first day and told his students they were guaranteed an "A" in the class. He told them they got an "A" just for registering. They wouldn't have to show up, they wouldn't have to do the assignments, they wouldn't have to participate in class lectures. If he never saw them again, they would still get an "A." He then said, "Now, stop worrying about the grade and let's focus on learning." He also told them that they didn't need to rate the class at the end since his ratings would be meaningless (he didn't want them to think the experiment was about padding his ratings).

Through this experiment, he wanted to create a safe place to learn and wanted to see if it made a difference for the students. He also wanted to eliminate the ever-present specter of judgment. He likened this experiment to life. Christ, in performing the Atonement, has given us the "A" and provided us a safe place to learn and grow. Because of His Atonement, He has created abundance. There's more than enough love for everyone, forgiveness for our mistakes, and compassion for suffering. There's more than enough because we are always good enough for Christ. There's an abundance of *good*. You are always worthy enough for His love. With grateful hearts, we can live in abundance believing Christ's abundance is infinite.

---

63. Gordon B. Hinckley, *Way to Be! 9 Rules For Living the Good Life* (United States: Simon & Schuster, 2002), 84.

Student attendance for the class that semester was as good or better than any other semester in the seventeen years Jeff taught. And student involvement in discussions, as well as homework being turned in and lab reports being completed, was as good as any other semester he taught. And before the final he reminded them they all had A's and taking the finals was unnecessary. Every student showed up and completed the final. The one student that came back to give Jeff a rating gave him a perfect score in every category. That student, for sure, had figured out the experiment.

I have found so many different tools to assist me in keeping an abundance mindset. The important point is to start by making the decision to change and then finding the tools that work for you. Jeff's path to abundance is so different from mine, but we have found that increasing in gratitude and trust is a common factor in moving toward abundance.

In the introduction we told you about how we sat down as a couple and made goals for a year, five years, ten years, fifteen years, and twenty years. As the years went by, we kept working on those goals. We tweaked them, refined them, and by the time we hit twenty years of marriage, we looked back at what we had created in our lives and recognized those goals aided us in living a life of abundance. We weren't perfect in achieving every single goal, but we were perfectly growing into what God intended us to become. We learned, struggled, evolved, and our life grew into "more than enough." We have more than enough love, more than enough time, more than enough energy, more than enough money, more than enough ideas, more than enough inspiration.

Each day as we design our life—no matter our circumstances—we are manifesting just what we desire to step into. The feelings of learning, growing, and achieving are exhilarating, but the biggest learning point is seeing, with immense gratitude, that when we made the creative statements—even 20 years in advance—we were manifesting our dreams. God is a God of Abundance and He helped us exceed our goals beyond our wildest dreams. "I am come that they might have life, and that they might have it more abundantly" (John 10:10). Jesus came so that I can live an abundant life. I get to lean into that and learn how to live more abundantly.

Every day I reflect on the fact that God is a God of Abundance. We learn this principle in our god training. The scriptures are filled with His example of abundance. Charity is an abundance of love. Prosperity is an abundance of blessings. "Prove me now herewith, saith the Lord of hosts, if I will not open you the windows of heaven and pour you out a blessing, that there shall not be room enough to receive it" (Malachi 3:10). Once again, God has created the pattern for me to follow.

I chose to conclude each chapter with a reference to the "Light Fountain," because, to me, the "Light Fountain" represents the Savior Jesus Christ, for He *is* "the light of the world" (John 8:12), and the "fountain of life" (Psalms 36:9). He invites all to drink of the waters of life freely (John 7:37, Revelation 21:6, D&C 10:66), and His Fountain is abundant—eternal.

Bringing It All Together

I HAVE FELT THE WINDOWS OF HEAVEN OPEN AS I HAVE LEANED INTO these principles. Each building on the other and intersecting in powerful ways that connect me to my Savior and His Atonement. I have felt His healing in connection. I have partnered as a co-creator with Him in designing and seeing beauty in my life, even in the ashes. He has restored my body, spirit, and mind, renewed my zest for life, and refreshed my perspective of the world. I feel Him walking with me, as I study His story and welcome Him in mine. I am able to find a holy place where I feel connection with Him and feel yoked with Him. Wherever I go I can stand on holy ground because I am in the Fountain of His Light, that is abundant and endless.

I feel privileged to have a chance to share these things with you and it truly has been fun to see these principles that I love so much and that have allowed me to have such a fulfilling life materialize in these pages. Jeff and I have shared parts of our journey that led us to know that we are the creators of our lives, but now this is about you and what you do with this knowledge. Join us on the mobile device

---

64. Thomas Keating, *Open Mind, Open Heart* (United States: Continuum, 1995), 128.

app, PRIXM. We have created a community there called DESIGN YOUR LIFE and we would love to connect with you and hear of your experiences as you design your life.

Now, I challenge you to go through the exercises in the included workbook with an open heart and mind. Work at your own pace to see all of the principles coming together in each exercise and feel the power to create something different, something new, something beautiful. Expand and deepen your connections to your true self, God, and others. See creativity from a new perspective and know that you are a creative being. Allow beauty to surround you by seeing it and by creating it. Infuse your life with fun and enthusiasm by making play a priority. Use your story to connect with the past, present, and future. Live life with reverence as you take the time to be still and tap into your authentic power. Step into an abundance mindset and feel your heart and mind expand.

Rise up and recognize that *you are the designer of your life!*

About the Authors

Rhonna and Jeff manage a successful design/app business and are two of the founders of a business that will change the way we record and maintain our life histories and store our memories. Rhonna is a creative graphic artist/designer that continually pushes the edge of digital design for personal histories, and Jeff is an imaginative scientist that can't keep his mind off the relationship between the physical world and consciousness.

Rhonna graduated from BYU with a degree in art education and came up with creative ways to keep the family prospering while Jeff worked toward a PhD in materials science and engineering. They love spending time with their grown children in their mountain home in Utah.

To learn more about Rhonna and Jeff, visit:
www.rhonnadesigns.com
www.prixm.com